English Debate Education
영어 토론 교육

임주영 지음

gb 지오북스

영어토론교육

초판발행 2021년 10월 9일

저　자 임주영
펴낸곳 지오북스
등　록 2016년 3월 7일 제395-2016-000014호
전　화 02)381-0706 | **팩스** 02)371-0706
이메일 emotion-books@naver.com
홈페이지 www.geobooks.co.kr

ISBN 979-11-91346-17-6
값 19,000원

이 책은 저작권법으로 보호받는 저작물입니다.
이 책의 내용을 전부 또는 일부를 무단으로 전재하거나 복제할 수 없습니다.
파본이나 잘못된 책은 바꿔드립니다.

이 책의 머리말

　이 책은 저자가 2009년부터 2010년까지 하버드 대학교(Harvard University)와 예일 대학교(Yale University)에서 있었던 국제토론교육에서 한국 대표 코치로 일했고, 2015년부터 2018년까지 한국뉴욕주립대학교(SUNY)에서 인천 교육청 중·고등학교 영어교사 연수에 매니저로 일했던 경험을 바탕으로 만들어지게 되었습니다. 이 책의 목적은 영어 교육 현장에서 활력이 넘치는 의사소통 중심의 교실영어 교육을 꾀하고 또 한편으로는 학습자의 논리적·비판적 사고를 향상시키고 영어토론 교육을 중점 교육하여 질 높은 우수한 영어교사 양성에 있습니다. 이 교재는 영어토론교사의 양성을 위해 Second language Acquisition 및 Language Teaching을 근간으로 한 실습중심의 실용영어교육과정을 강도 높게 교육하기 위해 구성되었습니다.

　언어의 꽃이라고 불리는 토론은 다양한 주제에 대해 찬성과 반대의 입장에서 자신들의 사고를 바탕으로 지니고 있던 지식과 경험, 의견을 비판적이고 논리적인 사고의 틀 안에서 서로 논쟁하며 논의하는 과정입니다. 그저 어리다고만 생각했던 우리 학생들의 사상과 생각 속에는 진지하고 논리적이며 비판적인 추리를 보유 하고 있습니다. 많은 분들이 토론의 주제가 때로는 무겁기에 깊은 배경 지식을 보유해야 한다고 생각하시지만, 학생들의 생각에 시동을 걸어주는 기폭제와 자극만 있다면 주제의 논리와 사실을 바탕으로 교사의 바람직한 리드를 통해 자신들의 생각을 표현하고 의견을 나눈다는 것은 생각보다 쉽고 빠르게 이루어 질 수 있습니다.

　학생들은 토론교육을 통해 다양한 주제에 대해 리서치하고 찬반으로 나뉘어 토론하다 보면 정해진 시간 안에 자신의 의견을 논리적으로 정리하고 효과적으로 발표하는 방법을 배우게 되고, 타인의 의견에 귀 기울여 경청하는 법을 배우게 됩니다. 영어토론이 가진 또 다른 장점은 영어를 폭 넓게 공부할 수 있도록 해준다는 것입니다. 물론, 영어를 사용하는 기회를 만드는 데 반드시 토론이란 틀이 필요한 것은 아닙니다. 하지만 영어토론의 틀을 사용하면

좀 더 쉽게 정치, 사회, 문화, 과학 등 다양한 주제에 대한 대화의 장을 열 수 있습니다. 토론에 참가할 사람들은 토론 주제에 대해 자신의 생각을 정리해야 하고 관련된 자료를 조사하여 토론에 대해 준비해야 합니다. 또한 다양한 주제에 대해서 글을 읽도록 유도할 수 있고 일상적인 대화에서는 사용하지 않던 전문 용어나 단어, 표현을 사용할 기회를 가지게 됩니다. 아울러, 영어토론을 통해서 영어권 나라들의 문화와 역사 등을 배워서 견문을 넓혀나갈 수 있습니다. 영어회화는 단순히 외국인과 직무를 수행함에 있어서 필요한 것일 때가 많고, 영어토론은 더욱 깊은 대화를 위해서 필요한 부분이라고 말할 수 있기 때문입니다.

마지막으로 영어토론을 가르치고자 하시는 영어 교사 분들께 이 책이 작으나마 영어토론의 기본을 이해하고 영어토론교육을 실제 교실에서 다양하게 활용할 수 있는 가이드북이 되기를 바랍니다. 그러기 위해서 학생들과 영어 교사 분들에게 실수를 두려워하지 말라고 주문하고 싶습니다. 실수에 대한 두려움이 토론에 참가하여 자기주장을 펼치는 것에 걸림돌이 되어서는 안 되기 때문입니다. 완벽한 영어를 구사하기 전까지 영어를 사용하지 않겠다는 마음가짐으로는 영원히 완벽한 영어를 구사할 수 없을 것이기 때문입니다. 많은 사람들과 다양한 주제를 가지고 입 주위의 근육이 얼얼하도록 영어로 토론하는 것은 영어 학습자에게 많은 도움이 되는 확실한 훈련이 될 것입니다. 다른 사람과 스포츠 경기를 하듯이, 자신만의 사유와 아집을 넘어서 영어를 통해 의견을 나누고 반성하는 것은 쉽게 할 수 없는 귀중한 경험이 될 것입니다.

영어토론은 영어 학습적인 면의 효과뿐만 아니라 토론 자체의 중요성을 생각해서도 이 시대에서 꼭 필요한 교육이 될 것입니다. 영어토론 교육을 통해 듣기, 읽기, 말하기, 쓰기의 훈련뿐 아니라 창의적, 비판적이고 논리적인 사고력을 향상시킬 수 있을 뿐 아니라 상대방에 대한 예의와 협동심을 기를 수 있게 되므로 최근 더욱 많은 사람들에게 그 교육적 중요성을 주목 받게 되었습니다. 아무쪼록 이 책이 영어토론교육을 통해 창의적 사고 능력과 의사소통 능력을 향상시켜서 미래 사회를 위한 우수한 인재들을 지도하는데 작게나마 도움이 되기를 바랍니다.

2021년 8월
저자 임 주 영

Preface

This book was written by experiences working as a representative Korean coach in international discussion education at Harvard University and Yale University from 2009 to 2010 and also as a manager for middle/high school English instructor training held by Incheon office of education at SUNY from 2015 to 2018. The purpose of this book is to promote active communication-based classroom English education while improving logical and critical thought of learners and cultivate high quality English instructors by focusing on English discussion education in the field of English education. This material is organized to provide more in-depth and practice-based real-life English education course based on the second language acquisition and language teaching.

Known as the gist of language, discussion is a course for people to argue and dispute over knowledge, experience, and opinion of each other according to their perspectives in the critical and logical framework in pros and cons on various topics. Seeming immature ideas and thoughts of students tend to contain sincere, logical, and critical inferences. Many people think how in-depth background knowledge is required as topics of discussion are serious upon occasion. However, students can relatively rapidly and conveniently express and share their opinions if properly led by instructors based on logics and facts of a theme if there are stimulant and momentum on their ideas.

Students tend to learn how to logically organize and efficiently present their opinions in a given time if they research and discuss various themes in pros and cons through discussion education and also to listen carefully to others. Another strength of English discussion is to make students more widely learn English. Of course, discussion is not inevitable to have an opportunity to learn English. However, if participating in discussion, it becomes much easier to communicate with others over many topics such as politics, society, culture, and science. Participants in the discussion are required to organize their thoughts on topics and prepare for the discussion by researching related data. In addition, discussion makes people read articles in various topics and also have an opportunity to use jargons, words, or expressions that are not used in normal conversation. Furthermore, people are able to expand their horizon learning culture and history of English-speaking countries through English discussion. Conversation in English is often necessary to work with foreigners, and English discussion is required for more in-depth conversation.

Lastly, I wish for this book to be helpful as a guide book for English instructors who teach English discussion to understand the basics of English discussion and diversely use English discussion education in the classroom. For this, I recommend students and English instructors not to be afraid of mistakes. Fear on mistakes shall not be an obstacle for them to participate in the discussion and present their opinion. It is impossible to speak English fluently forever without strong mind-set to learn English until people speak perfect English. Discussion where people argue with many others repeatedly and fervently in English for various topics will definitely be a helpful training for English learners. Sharing opinion in English and reflecting themselves over their own boundaries and limitations will be a precious experience.

English discussion will become inevitable education in terms of the effect of English learning and the importance of discussion in this era. It is available to improve listening, reading, speaking, and writing ability in English as well as to improve creative, critical, and logical way of thinking through English discussion education. At the same time, it is feasible to build courtesy and cooperation on others that English discussion has recently received much attention in the eyes of educational importance from many people. I sincerely wish for this book to be helpful improving creative way of thinking and communication skills and guiding outstanding talents in our society through English discussion education in the future.

August, 2021

Author Ju-young Lim

이 책의 목차

Chapter 1	Introduction to Debate	07
Chapter 2	Essay Writing for Debate	13
Chapter 3	Principles of Debate: Public Forum & Original Oratory	17
Chapter 4	Brainstorming & Developing Your Ideas	25
Chapter 5	Research & Discussion	33
Chapter 6	Rebuttals	39
Chapter 7	How to Make a Presentation Effectively	46
Chapter 8	English Debate Education I	59
Chapter 9	English Debate Education II	65
Chapter 10	Tips for Judging a Round of Public Forum Debate	70
Chapter 11	Practical Teaching Methods in Debate Classes	78
Chapter 12	Discussion About Effective Teaching English Debate Classes	87
Chapter 13	Coaching Debating	97

Chapter 14   Establishing a Debating Programme ·············· 100

Chapter 15   Managing a Debating programme ················ 103

Chapter 16   Brainstorming ··· 106

Chapter 17   Criticizing Debate ···································· 116

Chapter 18   Practicum for Teaching Debate ··················· 119

Chapter 1.
Introduction to Debate

What is debate?

Debate is a competitive speaking activity that involves two sides arguing the merits of a resolution in an attempt to convince the judge that their argument is best. This process of convincing the judge is done through both real world examples and persuasive arguments made by the debater.

Competitive debate has occurred in high schools around the worlds for over a century. Debate encourages students to formulate research and deliver arguments on a range of topics. Students who participate in debate often find the skills learned through the debate experience to be some of the most valuable skills used throughout their lives.

For well over a century, high schools have had competitive interscholastic discussions. Many professors consider debate to be a useful educational activity because it demands students to create, study, and deliver strong arguments on a variety of important themes.

There have been many distinct debate formats used in competitions. Students participate in a variety of styles, including Lincoln-Douglas, parliamentary, student congress, model United Nations, policy debate, and Public Forum debate. Each discussion format has its own set of advantages and disadvantages. Classic Debate is a new debate format created by a group of debate teachers from Minnesota.

Classic debate is intended to attract a large number of students to competitive debate. Two-student teams will compete over current events. From October to December, the debating season takes place. Students will discuss two distinct issues during the season. In August, debate professors will choose the first topic. The second topic will be decided by the students who are taking part.

Being on debate team

Participants in debate are members of a team because it is a competitive activity. The debate team is much like a typical sports team with practice, meets/tournaments, and coaches. Practices, meets/tournaments, and coaches are all part of the debate team's schedule. It takes roughly an hour to complete a debate round (one full debate). In each discussion, a judge chooses a winner depending on which side does a better job of defending their stance.

Public Forum debates are argued by teams of two (two debaters on each side for a total of four in each round of debate). Each member of the two-person team gives speeches and helps his or her partner the best they can.

Invitational events draw schools from all throughout the state during the debate season. Top teams are frequently recognized with awards based on their performance. The championship competition takes place towards the end of the year. Your coach will be able to provide you with more information about your competition schedule.

Debaters meet once a week to practice. The debate team uses practice time to prepare for competition, just like a soccer team does to go through plays, chat about forthcoming opponents, and overall hone their skills.

How long will all of this take? "It depends," is the ideal response. The average debater practices a couple of nights a week. Every competition takes place on Saturday and lasts until mid-afternoon. The time commitment is mostly determined by the goals and desires of each member. A team member can attend as many tournaments as he or she wants. To put it another way, debaters can, for the most part, plan their own timetables. This will differ depending on your coach's individual needs.

The benefits of debate

For most people who participate in competitive debate, it is both a demanding and satisfying sport. Being a member of the debate team comes with a slew of advantages.

Fun: The vast majority of the tens of thousands of students who participate in debate tournaments each year will tell you that they have a good time. Everyone's experience is unique, but the thrill of competition, the camaraderie of teammates, and the travel opportunities all contribute to making debate enjoyable.

Teammates: Building connections with teammates who share similar interests is another advantage of being engaged.

Public Speaking Skills: Most individuals have a natural aversion to public speaking; debate gives a safe setting in which to practice these abilities so that when you're called upon to speak in college or on the job, you'll be prepared to perform a fantastic job. This boosts your chances of succeeding in key employment or scholarship interviews.

Analytical Skills: The capacity to examine a situation objectively and suggest viable answers is priceless. Debate is the best teacher of this skill, which is possessed by high-level business executives and professionals.

Research Skills: Debate teaches you how to become a world-class researcher, from traditional library research to Internet research. Any college student will tell you how beneficial this is.

Listening & Note taking Skills: Debate demands you to become a good listener and take good notes. This allows pupils to improve their scores and learn more quickly.

For good reason, many of the country's top lawyers, corporate executives, doctors, engineers, and government officials participated in high school debate. Simply put, debate-related skills assist one in advancing and maintaining one's position. Persuasion is a highly valued skill, and there is no better way to develop it than via argument.

The Role of the Judge

A judge will be assigned to each debate round to determine which side performs the best job debating. The judge is to make his or her decision based on the arguments presented during the debate phase, not on personal feelings about the issues. A judge will usually take notes and do his or her best to follow all of your points. The judge will write a ballot explaining his or her judgment at the conclusion of the argument. Your ballot will be returned to you after the conclusion of the tournament.

The schools that participate in a debate competition recruit judges. Teachers, parents, past high school debaters, and other interested adults could be among them. Some judges have a lot of experience, but a lot of them don't. Undoubtedly, you will be dissatisfied by a judge's judgment at some time throughout your argument career. It's best to think your judge is doing his or her best. Remember that discussion is subjective, and various individuals will perceive it differently.

A very tight debate could be a challenge for your judge. What should they do if the debate appears to be a draw? There are a variety of ways to break a tie. Some judges give the team bonus points for better delivery. Because the positive has the benefit of the final statement, some judges give the tie to the negative.

Debate is a controlled exchange of ideas. You now have a better understanding of what it takes to be a member of the debate team. You may also be aware that a competitive debate round consists of two people on opposing sides of a contentious statement known as a resolution. A judge oversees the debate round and chooses a winner based on the arguments presented.

English Discussion Education Guidebook

Essay Writing for Debate

Three parts of essay

1. Introductory paragraph

The introduction introduces the topic and leads the audience/readers into the article. It should start with a hook that grabs the reader's attention. This hook could be a quote, a comparison, a question, or something else. The introduction should include some background information on the topic after grabbing the reader's attention. The ideas in the introduction should be broad enough for the audience/reader to understand the main assertion, then get more explicit as the thesis statement approaches. The introduction and thesis should each be one paragraph in length. The introduction should include the side of the resolution you are debating along with the resolution.

An introductory paragraph has two parts:

General statement: It is a main point or main idea of the essay, and it is a broad introduction to it's topic. It should capture the reader's interest by providing definition of something, settled facts, historical events, interesting story or statistics.

The thesis statement: It clearly identifies the topic being discussed, includes the points discussed in the paper, and is written for a specific audience. Your thesis statement belongs at the end of your first paragraph, also known as your introduction.

2. Body paragraph

The primary points offered in the thesis are supported by the essay's body. One or more paragraphs develop each point, which is backed up with concrete details. Depending on the project, this information may include research and personal experiences. In addition to this, the author's own study and discussion of the topic connects concepts and produces conclusions that back up the thesis.

The body paragraphs are a group of related sentences about a particular topic or relating to the thesis. in an essay are like the supporting sentences in a paragraph. You should organize body paragraphs according to some sort of pattern, such as a clear topic sentence, supporting details, and specific evidences.

Here are three keys to organizing a logical division essay:
1. Divide your thesis statement into topics, and then discuss each topic in a separate paragraph.
2. Write a thesis statement that indicates logical division.
3. Use transitions between paragraphs to guide your reader from one topic to the next. Every good paragraph has both unity and coherence:
1. You achieve unity by discussing only one main idea from beginning to the end in a paragraph. Always staying on the topic in your supporting sentences.
2. You achieve coherence (=hold together) by repeating key nouns, using consistent pronouns, using transition signals, arranging your ideas in some kind of logical

order.

3. Concluding paragraph

The conclusion brings all of the essay's important themes together. It returns to the thesis statement and provides readers with a final thought and sense of closure by resolving all of the essay's topics. It may also explore the argument's ramifications. New subjects or ideas that were not developed in the article should not be introduced in the conclusion.

The conclusion has three purposes.

1. It signals the end of the essay.
2. It reminds your reader of your main points, which you can do in one or two ways:
   1) You can summarize your subtopic
   2) Paraphrase your thesis. It leaves your reader with your final thoughts on the topic.
3. It leaves your reader with your final thoughts on the topic.

Unity and Coherence

The right essay and paragraph format not only helps you attain unity and consistency, but it also helps the reader understand what you're saying. Topic sentences and ending sentences that are well-written can also aid to keep the essay together.

Unity is the continuity of a single idea (the thesis) throughout the essay. Each detail and example should develop logically and refer back to the original focus.

Coherence means that each point should be linked to the previous and following points to help the essay flow and progress logically and clearly. An easy way to link paragraphs together is through transitions in each paragraph's topic sentence.

Essay Format

Introductory Paragraph : 1) General Statement

2) Thesis Statement

Body Paragraph ① : 1) Topic sentence

2) Supporting details

3) Specific evidence

Body Paragraph ② : 1) Topic sentence

2) Supporting details

3) Specific evidence

Body Paragraph ③ : 1) Topic sentence

2) Supporting details

3) Specific evidence

Concluding Paragraph : 1) Summarize your subtopic

2) Paraphrase your thesis

Chapter 3.
Principles of Debate: Public Forum & Original Oratory

1. Principles of Debate: Public Forum & Original Oratory

The 'Anatomy of an Argument'

A proper 'argument' has the following structure: An assertion is simply a statement of fact (or, in slightly more sophisticated terms, an assertion can include simplistic/superficial analysis ‑ see 'Casual Causation' below), whereas an assertion is simply a statement of fact (or, in slightly more sophisticated terms, an assertion can include simplistic/superficial analysis ‑ see 'Casual Causation' below).

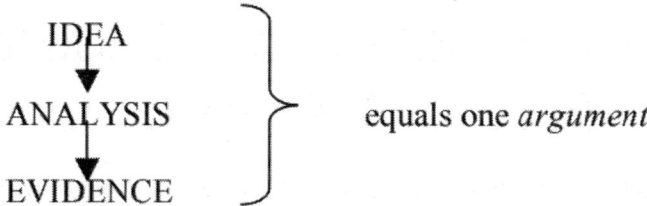

The various portions of an argument will be labeled differently by different persons, but this basic format is required for a correctly formulated argument.

IDEA stands for the concept or proposition that you are attempting to prove. It could be a principle, such as "the government has an obligation to provide free education," or it could simply be something that would be beneficial to your side of the debate, such as "the death penalty is an effective deterrent for criminals." In any case, it's meaningless on its own - it might be true or false. The point is that you and your team want people to believe that it's true.

So, how are you going to persuade them to believe it? So, you start with an ANALYSIS of why it's likely to be true - why believing it's true is logical and reasonable. This entails a lot of "why?" and "because" (out loud or in your brain)! But, in a moment, I'll give you an example.

Last but not least, there is the EVIDENCE. I put it last for two reasons: one, it's the least crucial, and second, it should be the last thing on your mind. Focus first on having the proper IDEAS about what your side needs to say, and then spend your time coming up with good analyses to make it sound logical. It's great if you have time after that to come up with evidence and examples.

Statistics (boring, but useful - such as the unemployment rate before and after a policy, or the percentage of individuals affected by a specific problem, or the costs of a proposal) or quotes can be used as evidence (not direct quotes, but knowing what important people have said about an issue).

2. Well prepare for the Debate

Remember your audience

Keep in mind who is in the room. As a senator, you have the option of giving up your time to audience members if you so want. Members in the audience may have a direct impact on the topic under discussion.

Organize the information

Content is what you actually say in the debate. The arguments used to develop your own side's case and rebut the opposite side's. The information on content is a general overview of what will be expected when you debate.

Communicate with body language sometimes

All eyes are on you at any speaking engagement or gathering. You are judged not only on what you say, but also on how you act. Pay attention to your opponent's nonverbal reactions to his or her assertion; an eye roll or pursed lips could appear unpleasant or aggressive. Also, keep in mind that you are being watched even if you are not speaking!

Deliver your message

Keep in mind that the purpose of any discussion or presentation is to persuade your audience that you, or your firm, and its products and services, are the best option. Mastering your subject and being able to articulate your ideas and arguments clearly can aid you in communicating your value statements and position in comparison to the competitors. Maintain your composure and actions to successfully show your authority and expertise on the subject.

Prepare thoroughly

To be credible as an expert on your subject and communicate intelligently, you must have a thorough comprehension of the subject and the ability to think on your feet. Knowing "your stuff" will help you be ready for anything comes your way. But knowing your arguments is only half of the battle. You must also be able to use sound arguments to counter the opposition. To be able to do so, you must first comprehend the opposing side's perspective.

3. Original Oratory

This is a memorized, persuasive speech, which attempts to convince, inspire, stimulate thinking, or move the listener to action. The subject should be of political, economic, social, or philosophic significance and should be limited to a specific topic. And original oratory is to be factual and researched. The speech has a time limits (typically ten minutes, but 3-5 minutes in classes) and can quote no more than 150 words.

The orator may use any suitable pattern of organization, which will provide a clear, logical development of his/her thesis. The oration should be the result of research, analysis, evaluation and personal conviction. An oration is not an essay. It is a speech. Thus, emphasis should be placed on oral communication and the student should remember that direct, communicative speech, not stilted or artificial delivery is their goal.

A clear voice, intonation, gestures, and specified movements (as transitions or for emphasis) add needed for it.

- The subject should be of political, economic, social, or philosophic significance and should be limited to a specific topic. And original oratory is to be factual and researched.
- The speech has a time limits (typically ten minutes, but 3-5 minutes in classes) and can quote no more than 150 words.
- The orator may use any suitable pattern of organization, which will provide a clear, logical development of his/her thesis.
- The oration should be the result of research, analysis, evaluation and personal conviction.
- An oration is not an essay: it is a speech. Thus, emphasis should be placed on oral communication and the student should remember that direct, communicative speech, not stilted or artificial delivery is their goal.
- A clear voice, intonation, gestures, and specified movements (as transitions or for emphasis) add needed for it.

4. Public Forum Debate

This is a team event that advocates or rejects a position posed by the monthly resolution topic. Topics are worded as resolutions, meaning they advocate solving a problem by establishing a position. A team must develop both a pro and con case, persuasively supported by evidence and reasoning. A team should research several arguments on both sides of the issue before the debate, so it can adapt its case to the opposing team's claims as necessary. A public forum debate consists of 8 speeches and 3 crossfires, each with a time limit.

5. Debate Structure

1. What is a Resolution?

In a debate, a resolution or topic is a normative statement which the affirmative team affirms and the negative team negates. The debate resolution is the focal point of the discussion. A resolution is a contentious statement that can be voted for or against. Resolutions might be factual, policy, or value statements. The positive team is always in favor of the resolution (affirms it). The resolution is opposed (negated) by the negative team.

A resolution may occasionally allow the affirmative team to decide. For instance, "Resolved that [Richard Nixon/Lyndon Johnson] was a better U.S. president." The affirmative must choose one of two choices to support in these "2-choice" resolutions. The negative must then back up the choice that the positive rejects.

The resolutions are chosen in order to foster lively debate. They should be fairly balanced in terms of positive and negative aspects (meaning that both sides should be able to make reasonable arguments). Good resolutions concentrate on important and current issues. They also make it easy for pupils to conduct research on the subject (topics that are obscure or topics that are too broad may present research difficulties).

2. Debate Argument Structure: Overview and Outline

Argument Structure for Debate

...and also the basic structure of all persuasive writing···.

While there are many forms of debate, a basic argument structure that will work in most debates is a CLAIM - REASON - EVIDENCE structure.

    1) Claim (Argument)

    2) Reason (Why?)

    3) Evidence (Proof)

...and also the basic structure of all persuasive writing….

CLAIM/OPINION - Is your argument expressed in one simple and clear sentence. This is not a restatement of the debate topic, this is one reason why you are in favor (PRO) the debate topic statement or one reason why you are against (CON) the debate topic statement. You may (and usually will) have multiple claims to support your side. A typical opening speech has three claims.

REASON - Is the reason why your argument matters. Your information may be true, but you need to go further to explain how this proves your point. This shows you're the logical thinking.

EVIDENCE - Is the evidence or proof that you are using to support your claim. Evidence often comes in the form of a quotation, statistics/data, or cited reference but also can include powerful examples or analogies.

6. Practice of Debate Basic Organization

<Example 1>

- Support your opinion with strong reasons and supports.
- Resolution: The country life is better than the city life.

    1) Claim - I agree with the resolution that the country life is better than the city life.

    2) Reason - The country is cleaner than the city.

    3) Support - The country is less polluted because there are fewer factories and fewer cars.

<Example 2>

- Resolution: Students should not wear uniforms at school.

    1) Claim - I agree with the resolution that students should not wear uniforms at school.

    2) Reason - School uniforms are not comfortable.

    3) Support - When they wear uniforms at school, the range of action done by students is very limited.

Chapter 4.
Brainstorming & Developing Your Ideas

What is Brainstorming?

The basic definition…but wait…there's more… So what do we choose?

(K.I.S.S.) ‑ keep it seriously simple

Brainstorming is coming up with many ideas (new, old, good, "bad") about a topic or challenge. It should involve coming up with ideas that are not always traditional or "what we always do"

Brainstorming realizes that our brains are "pattern recognition systems" and that we can get "stuck"

- so we need not be confined to a box

Breaking the Pattern of Programmed Thinking

Programmed Thinking is using a structure or traditional method to create something. Instead…

Lateral Thinking is about jumping outside of traditional patterns that we use to come up with ideas

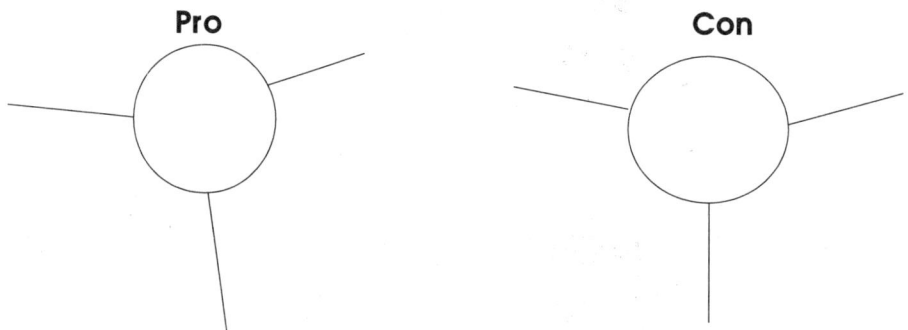

What do we want to accomplish?

- Define what brainstorming is and why it is important for a debate
- Look at basic techniques for brainstorming
- Understand when we use brainstorming
- Learn how to prepare ourselves for a debate, using brainstorming
- Next steps (how do we make sure we use brainstorming)

What is brainstorming?

Brainstorming is quickly writing down all the thoughts that come into your head. When you brainstorm, you do not think about whether your idea is good or bad or whether your idea is correct. You simply write to put your ideas on paper. This process is called brainstorming because it feels like there is a storm in your brain — a storm of ideas!

With brainstorming, we use this lateral approach to "find" ideas...

Brainstorming entails leveraging synergy — we pool our combined intelligence to generate a number of viable solutions. It is, however, difficult to have unrestricted freedom. Introverts may remain quiet in groups while extroverts dominate. The session leader must "police" the team to establish a healthy, solution-focused environment in which even the most reticent participants will speak up. A warm-up activity, such as asking participants to list ways the world might be different if metal were rubber, can help alleviate brainstorming "constipation."

Another danger is allowing the team to get off track and/or deal with other issues. Because we can employ brainstorming in any phase of the design process, even areas connected to a project's major scope, it's critical that participants stay focused on the problem at hand (what Osborn referred to as the "Point of View"). Similarly, framing challenges with "How Might We" queries reminds us that brainstorming is natural and unrestricted. Overall, your team should remain flexible in their hunt for solutions to problems rather than chasing a "holy grail" solution offered by someone else. The concept is to mine idea "ore" and polish "golden" solutions later.

- Think about everything that happens with a tornado (all the objects flying around) — that is brainstorming...

Well how do I know if I am doing it right?

The key is to make sure you find method best for you…

- Settle on some rules to help you
- Relaxed atmosphere
- No criticism or judgments
- Quantity matters
- All ideas are legitimate
- All ideas are put on the "sheet" of paper
- Evaluate only after the session

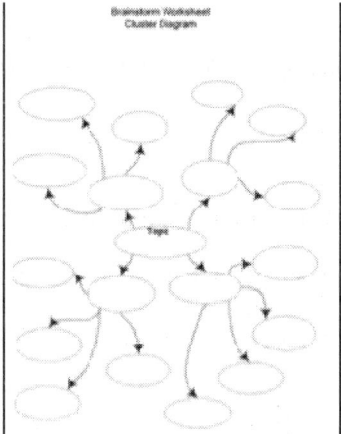

Notes:

Not ONLY ONE Way to Brainstorm

http://www.verticalmeasures.com/content/six-creative-ways-to-brainstorm-ideas/

Resources for Brainstorming

- Apps and Programs:
- Evernote (https://evernote.com)
- Penultimate (https://evernote.com/penultimate/)
- bubbl.us (https://bubbl.us)
- MagicalPad (http://www.magicalpad.com)
- Hotlist (http://mashable.com/2013/09/25/mind-mapping-tools/)
- Pen and Paper
- Always have something to write down your ideas (digitally or "old school")
- See what others have done (Google/Naver)

The visual brainstorming techniques we'd be looking at are

- **Mind Maps:** Mind maps are a tool used to visualize and organize information. Capturing your free flow of ideas using a mind map during brainstorming will help you quickly make sense of the relationships between the information you come up with. They are also a great way to break down an idea and analyze it.
- **Flowcharts:** A flowchart is a type of diagram that represents a workflow or process. A flowchart can also be defined as a diagrammatic representation of an algorithm, a step-by-step approach to solving a task.
- **SWOT Analysis:** SWOT analysis is a summary tool that lets you analyze the internal (Strengths and Weaknesses) and external (Opportunities and Threats) factors of your business.
- **Starbursting:** Starbursting gets you and your team to examine the problem first by asking not just the 6 key question(who, when, what, where, why, how), but also several other questions as necessary.
- **Fishbone Diagrams:** Fishbone diagrams, which is typically used to find the causes of an effect (hence named cause and effect diagram), can be used to facilitate a reverse brainstorming session.
- **Affinity Diagrams:** Affinity diagrams allow you to neatly arrange and group ideas so that it would be easy to read and analyze.
- **Concept Maps:** Concept maps are a learning and teaching technique that is used to identify the relationships between ideas or concepts. They help properly structure thoughts that are thrown around in a brainstorming session in a way that is easier to understand.

Are pros and cons really important?

- Original Oratory (Persuasive Speaking) Debate: In Original Oratory (Persuasive Speaking), students prepare and deliver an original speech designed to inspire, reinforce or change the beliefs, attitudes, values or actions of the audience.
- Classroom Debate Classroom debate can be a combination of many different debate styles. What is key to debating is being able to provide evidence that supports an opinion, while minimizing evidence that is unfavorable to your side of the issue. Developing skills to brainstorm ideas of pros and cons are essential to successful debate and having a resolution of the topic.

Let's try some practice.

- Read and understand the topic
- Brainstorm about the topic in the box
- Circle the ideas you think would be the best for your purpose

Topic: Terrifying Events

Brainstorm area:

The example of debating brainstorming

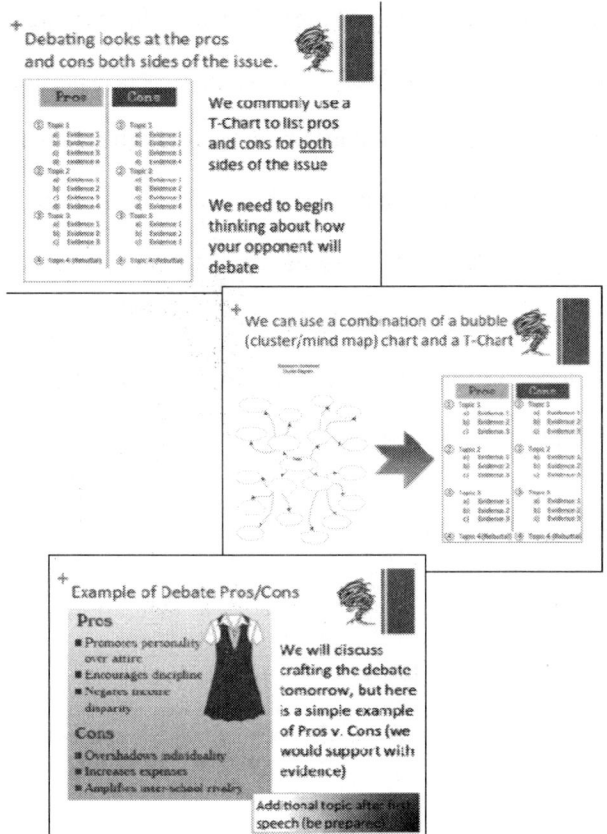

Chapter 5. Research & Discussion

Importance of Research

- For a Debater, knowledge is power.
- No matter how eloquent or passionate a speech may be, it will ultimately be toothless without key information and evidence to support the argumentation.
- Debaters will have to be well-read and well-researched if they are to improve in the debating arena.
- Diligent research will provide not only the evidence for cases but also generate the argumentation which can be used in debates.
- Arguments has to be based on facts, statistics, quotations, cases, and examples.
- Be prepare for the rebuttal argument as well.
- Use quality sources, such as peer-reviewed journals and academic books, to gather the best information possible about your debate topic.

Looking for information

- Internet
    - Online databases
    - Current information (online newspapers, articles, studies…)
- Library
    - Books
    - Periodicals
    - Government documents
    - Newspapers
    - Videos/DVDs
    - Human expertise

> ★ **10 Researching Tips for Debaters!**
> - Start with general search terms.
> - Compile articles first, then read them.
> - Don't go into research with a position in mind, at least in the preliminary stages.
> - Use as general search terms.
> - Keep a running list of positions.
> - Research in small stints.
> - Read the abstract first.
> - Don't shy away from graphs/tables/data.
> - Make a template.
> - Have a good research playlist.

"The greatest part of a writer's time is spent in reading, in order to write: a man will turn over half a library to make one book."

Samuel Johnson, The Life of Samuel Johnson

How to use search engines, including Google, effectively?

1) Initial Research

- **Choosing and combining search terms**
  - Define the subject in one sentence
    - The impact of coastal pollution in Britain
  - Split this sentence into concepts, discarding words which merely describe the relationship between one concept and another
    - Coastal Pollution Britain
  - For each of the concepts think of synonyms or related terms
    - Coastal – coast, coasts, beach, beaches
    - Pollution – oil, sewage
    - Britain – United Kingdom, UK, England, Scotland, Wales…
- **Combining search terms in your searches**
  - And: use AND if you want to retrieve references that contain both of the terms you are using.
    - E.g. Pollution AND Oil spills
  - - Or: Use OR if you want to retrieve references that contain either one of the terms you are using, or both terms together
    - E.g. Pollution OR Oil spills
- **Combining search terms in your searches**
  - Not: use NOT if you want to exclude references that contain a particular term
    - E.g. Pollution NOT Oil spills
  - Brackets: also many databases allow you to use brackets to make more complicated

searches
- E.g. (Pollution OR Oil) AND Seabirds
- Phrases: many databases allow you to search for phrases
- "Oil pollution"

2) Go Beyond Google

- ERIC (Education Resources Information Center)
- Education Research Complete
- Academic Search Elite
- Professional Development Collection
- SOCIdex
- Daily Life Online
- E-STAT (Government Statistics)
- EndNote (free 30-day trial version)
- DMOZ
- Google Scholar

Evidence

- Gather at least three pieces of evidence to support your claim
- Have information on each "sub topic" prepared ahead of time

Research Process

1) <u>Formulate research questions.</u> Before you begin any research, you should identify the questions you are trying to answer. It is important to identify research questions rather than topics. A question gives you a specific goal, whereas a topic is too open-ended.

2) <u>Select a method.</u> There are a variety of ways to find answers to your questions. Students who try various sources usually find more success and end up with deeper research. Some good methods include: article databases, specific internet sites, general internet searches, printed materials in the library, books, personal interviews.

3) <u>Keep trying.</u> Most likely, you won't succeed right away. Research takes perseverance. If you are not having any luck answering your questions, try new a different method, different key words, or ask for help. Often, you will need to try several different key words before you get what you want. Write down what you have tried and keep going.

4) <u>Have a system for recording your results</u>. Always have a notebook to jot down notes. Furthermore, make sure you are getting full source citations. If you are printing or copying articles, it is a good idea to staple and file them together and write the full citation on the top right away.

Why you must go beyond Google?

- Information 'hidden' for search engines
- Quality of information
- Quantity of information
- Limited search options

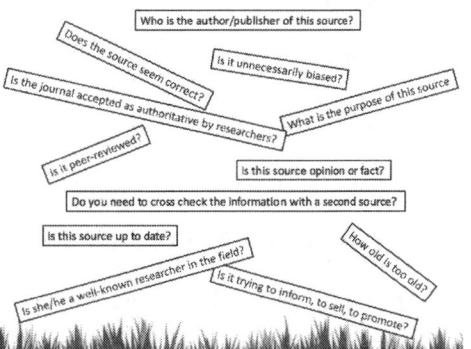

Evaluate your sources

- Think critically about the information you find. Remember that your opponent will be as well.
- Ask yourself questions…

Chapter 5 Research & Discussion

Weak evidence vs. strong evidence

- Make sure every statement is cited or referenced
    - It is better to spank children. (weak evidence)
    - Studies made by Child Abuse Prevention Association (CAPA) have shown that spanking children is an effective means of behavioral modification and that if used properly, leads to a better disciplined and more socially productive adult.
        (stronger evidence)

Examples of evidence

1) **Fact:** Traditionally favored by private and parochial institutions, school uniforms are being adopted by US public schools in increasing numbers.

2) **Statistics:** About one in five US public schools (21%) require students to wear uniforms. 25% percent of primary schools have student uniforms, compared to 20% of middle schools and 12% of high schools.

3) **Quotation:** Frank Quatrone, superintendent in the Lodi district of New Jersey, stated that "When you have students dressed alike, you make them safer. If someone were to come into a building, the intruder could easily be recognized."

4) **Case:** A study by the University of Houston found that elementary school girls' language test scores increased by about three percentile points after uniforms were introduced.

5) **Example:** Typically, uniforms are more expensive up-front, as the parent must invest in all of the staples at the beginning of the school year, for example, there are collared or polo shirts of various colors, khaki or black pants, black or brown belts, and shoes, and solid colored sweaters.

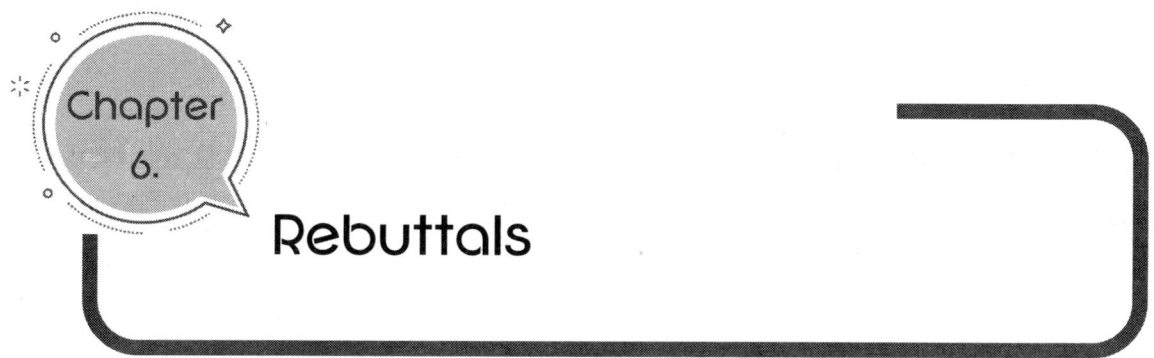

Chapter 6. Rebuttals

1. What is rebuttal in debate?

- Rebuttal is an essential element of debating – it provides the "clash of ideas" that makes debating different from public speaking. Rebuttal requires debaters to listen to what is being said by the other side and respond to their arguments.

2. What make you a good rebuttal?

- Rebuttal is where you explain the flaws in the other team's arguments. The most effective rebuttals will attack the core of an opposition's argument as being ILLOGICAL or IRRELEVANT to the topic, and it is always better to attack the argument itself rather than the example or evidence they use to back it up.

3. What should a rebuttal consist of?

- By addressing and challenging each aspect of a claim, a rebuttal provides a counter-argument, which is itself a type of argument. In the case of a rebuttal essay, the introduction should present a clear thesis statement and the body paragraphs should provide evidence and analysis to disprove the opposing claim.

4. 5 Effective Tips for Writing a Good Academic Rebuttal Letter

1) Be Polite and Respectful.

2) Provide Point-by-Point Replies to All the Referees' Comments.

3) Highlighting Changes in Your Manuscript.

4) Choose the Right Ending.

5) Becoming a Reviewer.

5. 5 frequent faults with arguments that anyone should be able to recognize regardless of how much they know about a topic

1. **Assertion** - the argument isn't really an argument at all; it's just a statement, and there's no logical reason to assume it's correct. Simply state why there hasn't been any/enough analysis to support the assertion's validity, and then explain why the assertion isn't obvious or intuitively correct.

2. **Contradiction** - Although the argument is valid, it contradicts a preceding argument. It must be the case that the two arguments in question cannot both be true at the same time to constitute a true − or 'full blown' − contradiction. As a result, it is illogical to think that doing something is both cheaper and more expensive. You'll appear silly if you start calling every argument you hear a contradiction. If it is a contradiction, it can do a lot of harm to your opponent's argument; if it isn't, the false accusation can do a lot of damage to your credibility!

But spotting – and pointing out – a contradiction is only the beginning, if you want to fully exploit it you have to explain to the adjudicator exactly how this compromises the credibility of their case. So don't just state "originally they said their plan would be incredibly inexpensive, and now they say it will be really expensive, but it will be worth the money - that's a pretty clear contradiction," add some analysis, such as "so which is it then?" One of them clearly doesn't grasp the gravity of the situation – if a low-cost program can be effective, why is she trying to convince us that we'll need to spend a lot of money to solve the problem? If she's correct, and it'll take a lot of money to make a dent in this problem, then everything the first guy said is nonsense. Hopefully, their next speaker will reveal which of his teammates knows what they're talking about, and which is just making things up." You should try to make them as uncomfortable as possible, and push them to not only withdraw the assertion, but also admit that some of their reasoning are useless.

As you can see, a contradiction is a very serious problem in a case, thus if your team is accused of running a contradiction, it is critical that you answer as soon as possible and seek to show how the two arguments are not contradictory.

3. Casual Causation – Essentially this is a lack of analysis. It occurs when someone tries to draw a link between two events, without showing how the former event actually caused the latter event to happen.

People who say that introducing the death penalty for murderers reduces the frequency of murders is a classic example. Leaving aside the fact that the introduction of the death penalty has been linked to an increase in the murder rate, there is simply no reason to believe that the death penalty is a deterrent.

4. False Dichotomy – This a particular type of mischaracterization of a debate or problem. It occurs when someone says that there is a choice to be made, where the only options are 'A' or 'B', when in fact they are not the only choices available.

This can happen when a speaker is attempting to establish a self-serving dichotomy (in effect, "this debate/argument is a choice between doing something positive to address this problem, or simply letting things get worse" - in a decent debate, this will almost never be the case; it will almost always be a choice between two options designed to improve a situation). Alternatively, a speaker may provide a false dichotomy because they are stupid/lazy and do not fully comprehend the debate/your point.

In either case, it's critical to recognize when someone is seeking to divide the debate into two camps, one of which is either not what you're arguing for or not what anyone would argue for. Keep in mind what your team is trying to show at all times, and you should be able to handle this circumstance with ease.

5. **Straw Man** - This is another type of misrepresentation or mischaracterization of an argument. Basically, the straw man is when a team set up an argument (which you have not made, and don't intend too) and then proceed to rebut it.

This might happen when a speaker uses an extreme example of your idea, when they distort anything you stated, or when they expected you to argue a specific way but instead presented something slightly different. It doesn't matter why; it's critical to call out when a team isn't engaged with your case, since if you let a straw man argument be hammered to death without pointing out that it wasn't your argument in the first place, a weak adjudicator might conclude it was. It's also crucial to point out when your opponents aren't participating, as this is a vital element of having a productive argument.

6. A rebuttal has two dynamics…

It is a battlefield where you need to both attack the opponent and defend yourself verbally.

What to do in a rebuttal − it is a refuting of your opponent's proposals/arguments:

7. The goal of refutation is to answer your opponent's arguments:

1) Identifying the particular argument you are refuting
2) Critically evaluating the argument and explaining why it is wrong
3) Supplying additional evidence to support your claims
4) Explaining the implications of this particular argument for the more controversial issue

Notes:

8. 7 ways to critically react to an argument

1) A request for clarification, explanation or elucidation may contain an implicit criticism that the argument was not clearly expressed.

2) A challenge to an argument comprises an expression of critical doubt about whether a reason supports the argument.

3) A bound challenge raises a more specific doubtful point that offers some reason for entertaining doubt.

4) An exposure of a flaw poses a negative evaluation of an argument and requests further amplification.

5) Rejection is a kind of critical reaction by an opponent who may not deny that the proponent's argument is reasonable, but takes up an opposite point of view.

6) A charge of fallacy criticizes the contribution of the proponent by claiming he or she has violated some rule of fair procedure.

7) A personal attack is a common kind of critical reaction that provides a means of defence against unreasonable moves by one's opponent.

Notes:

9. Useful Debating Phrases

- But before I come to my own arguments, let us first have a look at what ⋯ has said
- I will continue our case in a minute, but before that there are some things about the ⋯ speech that need to be addressed
- He/She also said that ⋯; but in fact ⋯
- He/She was claiming that ⋯; but as my first speaker already told you, ⋯

10. Rebuttal and Reconstruction (http://idebate.org/training/resources/136)

- Developing Counterpoints
- Rebuttal Re-do
- Refutation and Impact Back
- Refutation Ball
- Refutation in Four Movements
- Repetition, Assertion, Deviation

Chapter 7. How to Make a Presentation Effectively

To clarify, the following text discusses the ins and outs of creating good debate presentations to support your case:

- To begin, thoroughly organize your data and include all supporting evidence. Get as far as you can into your research for your presentation in order to obtain up-to-date statistics to support your case.

- Following the collecting of facts, it is time to organize the information in a way that is beneficial to you. Using metaphors and phrases can be advantageous! However, avoid facts about which you are unsure.

- Keep an eye on your body language during the presentation; it should be neither provocative nor relaxing. But don't lose your cool! Your body language and tone of speech must constantly convey a positive message.

- There is one additional factor in arguments that needs your attention: presence of mind. Always be aware of your surroundings, listen to what others have to say, and be prepared to improvise your presentation on the fly. React promptly and effectively in general.

- The conclusion must have the same impact as the opening. Make sure that at the conclusion of your debate, your audience is given some homework.

The conclusion must have the same impact as the opening. Make sure that at the conclusion of your debate, your audience is given some homework.

Steps for Planning and Drafting Your Speech

1. **Clarify your position.** How do you feel about the issue and why?

2. **Find support for your position.** What research will you have to do back up your case? Where can you find that information? Which evidence will help you make you point most effectively?

3. **Identify your audience.** What do your listeners already know about the issue? What is their stand on it?

4. **Consider how to grab your listeners' attention.** What starting statistics, amusing anecdotes, or intriguing questions can you use to hook your audience at the beginning?

5. **Decide how to present your arguments.** How can you organize your arguments so they have the greatest impact? Do you want to begin with the argument your audience will probably agree with and move to more controversial points? Would starting with the strongest argument – or ending with it – work better?

Guidelines & Standard of Persuasive Speech

\<Content\>

A successful persuasive speech should

- open with a clear statement of the issue and your opinion
- be geared to the audience you're trying to persuade
- provide facts, examples, statistics, and reasons to support your opinion
- answer opposing views
- show clear reasoning
- include strategies such as frequent summaries to help listeners remember your message
- end with a strong restatement of your opinion or a call to action

\<Delivery\>

There are at least two prerequisites for effective debate. To begin, a debater must have strong arguments. Second, a debater must be able to successfully express his or her points to the judge or the audience. This chapter focuses on effective communication.

Articulation

Let's start with the fundamentals. You are not communicating successfully if the audience does not understand what you are saying. To articulate properly, you must speak clearly and pronounce your words correctly.

Problems with articulation to look out for:

- Mumbling or Slurring (this is usually a result of not pronouncing words carefully).
- Common grammatical errors ('gonna' instead of going to, 'cuz' instead of because, etc.)

Volume

Every speaking situation necessitates the speaker adjusting his or her volume to fit the situation. Of course, a speaker must be loud enough for the audience to hear him or her properly. The audience, on the other hand, will grow annoyed or uncomfortable if a speaker speaks too loudly. To accentuate specific essential points, it is a good idea for a speaker to adjust his or her loudness during the speech. A minor rise or decrease in volume might draw attention to a key point made by the speaker.

Rate

Your rate of speech, like volume, can be excessively rapid or too sluggish. The audience will be bored by a very slow discourse. On the other hand, if the delivery is excessively fast, the listener will miss essential aspects or perhaps tune out. Different speaking situations necessitate different rates. The tempo of delivery utilized by television news reporters is a useful model for debaters. Listen to a CNN anchor for a notion of an ideal delivery rate.

Debaters will sometimes speak quickly in order to get more information into their speeches. This has been taken to an extreme in some debating settings. Debaters in various forms have employed incredibly quick delivery because the judges are not evaluating speakers on their delivery skills. Judges in Classic Debate, on the other hand, are particularly instructed to assess students' delivery as well as their arguments.

Vocal Variety

When you speak clearly and at the appropriate rate and volume, you ensure that the listener hears you. What more can you do to entice them to pay attention? Vocal diversity is one of the most important factors. Monotone (or dull!) is a term used to describe a speaker who does not vary his or her delivery. You can change the tone of your voice by changing the loudness or the rate. You can also alter the pitch and tone of your voice. This is referred to as inflection. Using pauses of varying lengths might also make your speech simpler to follow.

Posture and Gesture

You want your audience to perceive you as professional, at ease, and assured. You should pay attention to your posture and gestures in order to project a positive picture. The first rule is to avoid doing anything that would cause your audience to become distracted. Standing up straight with your feet aimed toward your audience is proper speaking posture. Slouching, leaning on walls or tables, and pointing your feet to one side or the other are all bad habits to avoid.

Gestures, on the other hand, are more difficult to learn. To begin with, what you have in your hands—evidence or notes—might obstruct your gestures. This is regarded to be a topic of discussion. When you've mastered the art of gesturing, there are a few common guidelines to follow:

- Always make a gesture above the trash can.
- Use a gesture to emphasize a point. Your movements should be deliberate.
- Make a variety of gestures. Avoid using the same gestures again and over.

Eye Contact

If at all feasible, look your audience in the eyes. You'll have to look down at your notes and evidence, of course. At the same time, avoid looking down for the most of your speech. Speakers who look their audience in the eyes are more compelling, according to research. Your audience may also provide you with valuable nonverbal feedback that you may use to improve your speech. Is the audience engaged, perplexed, unable to hear you, or agreeing with you? Looking at your audience can teach you a lot. You should spend time staring at each individual in the audience if there are more than one.

Appearance

Many people believe that your physical appearance has a role in your delivery. The dress code for various debating tournaments varies. You may be required to dress professionally on occasion (like you would for a business interview). At other times, you'll be expected to dress more casually. Your coach will offer advice on how to prepare for competition. Always keep in mind that your look has an effect on the audience. Your clothing conveys a statement. What is the message you wish to convey? Practice, practice, practice! It is possible to improve delivery at any time. Practice can be done in a number of ways. You can rehearse by giving the same speech numerous times and focusing on improving your delivery. You can practice with your teammates by assisting each other in the evaluation process. You can also work with a coach, instructor, or parent to improve your skills. Simply present your speech and seek comments on how well it was delivered. Alternatively, enlist assistance with a specific aspect of delivery. The more you practice, the more proficient you'll become.

- convey enthusiasm and confidence
- stand with good, but relaxed, posture and make eye contact with the audience
- include gestures and body language to enhance the presentation

A successful presenter should

- Convey enthusiasm and confidence
- Stand with good, but relaxed, posture and make eye contact with the audience
- Include gestures and body language to enhance the presentation

Writing and Delivering Your Persuasive Speech

1. Planning and drafting to find topic ideas for your speech:
- Make a list of things you feel strongly about.
- Brainstorming with friends about issues that you often debate.

2. Practicing and Delivering
- The best way to practice your speech is to present it aloud – again and again.
- Try speaking in front of a mirror so you an evaluate and improve your posture, gestures, eye contact.
- You might record a practice session so you can critique your voice quality and effectiveness.

3. Practicing and Delivering
- Responding to audience feedback.

Ex. 1: I couldn't remember the points you made.

> Include frequent summaries and reminders such as "I've just shown that you should believe X for reason A. My second reason for believing X is..."

Ex.2: I couldn't hear you.

> Speak loudly, but don't shout. Be sure to vary your volume and tone. Try to speak clearly and not too quickly.

Ex. 3: Your evidence didn't convince me.

> Gather additional expert opinions, facts, statistics, and examples; reorganize your arguments; check your reasoning.

Ex. 4: I was bored.

> Include an interesting quotation or personal anecdote; change the pace and volume of your voice; move around the room.

Writing and Delivering Your Persuasive Speech

① Planning and Drafting to find topic ideas for your speech:
- Make a list of things you feel strongly about.
- Brainstorming with friends about issues that you often debate.

② Practicing and Delivering
- The best way to practice your speech is to present it aloud ‐ again and again.
- Try speaking in front of a mirror so you an evaluate and improve your posture, gestures, eye contact.
- You might record a practice session so you can critique your voice quality and effectiveness.

③ Revising
- Responding to audience feedback.

- I couldn't remember the points you made.
  => Include frequent summaries and reminders such as "I've just shown that you should believe X for reason A. My second reason for believing X is..."
- I couldn't hear you.
  => Speak loudly, but don't shout. Be sure to vary your volume and tone. Try to speak clearly and not too quickly.
- Your evidence didn't convince me.
  => Gather additional expert opinions, facts, statistics, and examples; reorganize your arguments; check your reasoning.
- I was bored.
  => Include an interesting quotation or personal anecdote; change the pace and volume of your voice; move around the room.

Organization & Structure

1. Introduction: Establish audience interest and attention, preview thesis/ main points
2. The Body: Limit division of main points to 3 to 5 sub-points, use good transitions, order points in a way that is easy to understand and remember
3. The Conclusion: Review main points, remind audience why the subject is important to them

Tips for Effective Presentations

1. Show your Passion and Connect with your Audience.

- It's hard to be relaxed and be yourself when you're nervous. But time and again, the great presenters say that the most important thing is to connect with your audience, and the best way to do that is to let your passion for the subject shine through. Be honest with the audience about what is important to you and why it matters. Be enthusiastic and honest, and the audience will respond.

2. Focus on your Audience's Needs.

- Your presentation needs to be built around what your audience is going to get out of the presentation. As you prepare the presentation, you always need to bear in mind what the audience needs and wants to know, not what you can tell them. While you're giving the presentation, you also need to remain focused on your audience's response and react to that. You need to make it easy for your audience to understand and respond.

3. Keep it Simple: Concentrate on your Core Message.

- When planning your presentation, you should always keep in mind the question: What is the key message (or three key points) for my audience to take away? You should be able

4. Smile and Make Eye Contact with your Audience.

- This sounds very easy, but a surprisingly large number of presenters fail to do it. If you smile and make eye contact, you are building rapport, which helps the audience to connect with you and your subject. It also helps you to feel less nervous, because you are talking to individuals, not to a great mass of unknown people.

5. Start Strongly.

- The beginning of your presentation is crucial. You need to grab your audience's attention and hold it. They will give you a few minutes' grace in which to concentrate them before they start to switch off if you're dull. Start with a shocking fact, statistics etc.

6. Tell Stories: Human beings are programmed to respond to stories.

- Human beings are programmed to respond to stories. Stories help us to pay attention, and also to remember things. If you can use stories in your presentation, your audience is more likely to engage and to remember your points afterwards. It is a good idea to start with a story, but there is a wider point too: you need your presentation to act like a story.

5 frequent faults with arguments that anyone should be able to recognize regardless of how much they know about a topic

1. Assertion - the argument isn't really an argument at all; it's just a statement, and there's no logical reason to assume it's correct. Simply state why there hasn't been any/enough analysis to support the assertion's validity, and then explain why the assertion isn't obvious or intuitively correct.

2. Contradiction - Although the argument is valid, it contradicts a preceding argument. It must be the case that the two arguments in question cannot both be true at the same time to constitute a true – or 'full blown' – contradiction. As a result, it is illogical to think that doing something is both cheaper and more expensive. You'll appear silly if you start calling every argument you hear a contradiction. If it is a contradiction, it can do a lot of harm to your opponent's argument; if it isn't, the false accusation can do a lot of damage to your credibility!

But spotting – and pointing out – a contradiction is only the beginning, if you want to fully exploit it you have to explain to the adjudicator exactly how this compromises the credibility of their case. So don't just state "originally they said their plan would be incredibly inexpensive, and now they say it will be really expensive, but it will be worth the money - that's a pretty clear contradiction," add some analysis, such as "so which is it then?" One of them clearly doesn't grasp the gravity of the situation – if a low-cost program can be effective, why is she trying to convince us that we'll need to spend a lot of money to solve the problem? If she's correct, and it'll take a lot of money to make a dent in this problem, then everything the first guy said is nonsense. Hopefully, their next speaker will reveal which of his teammates knows what they're talking about, and which is just making things up." You should try to make them as uncomfortable as possible, and push them to not only withdraw the assertion, but also admit that some of their reasoning are useless.

As you can see, a contradiction is a very serious problem in a case, thus if your team is accused of running a contradiction, it is critical that you answer as soon as possible and seek to show how the two arguments are not contradictory.

3. Casual Causation – Essentially this is a lack of analysis. It occurs when someone tries to draw a link between two events, without showing how the former event actually caused the latter event to happen.

People who say that introducing the death penalty for murderers reduces the frequency of murders is a classic example. Leaving aside the fact that the introduction of the death penalty has been linked to an increase in the murder rate, there is simply no reason to believe that the death penalty is a deterrent.

4. False Dichotomy – This a particular type of mischaracterization of a debate or problem. It occurs when someone says that there is a choice to be made, where the only options are 'A' or 'B', when in fact they are not the only choices available.

This can happen when a speaker is attempting to establish a self-serving dichotomy (in effect, "this debate/argument is a choice between doing something positive to address this problem, or simply letting things get worse" – in a decent debate, this will almost never be the case; it will almost always be a choice between two options designed to improve a situation). Alternatively, a speaker may provide a false dichotomy because they are stupid/lazy and do not fully comprehend the debate/your point.

In either case, it's critical to recognize when someone is seeking to divide the debate into two camps, one of which is either not what you're arguing for or not what anyone would argue for. Keep in mind what your team is trying to show at all times, and you should be able to handle this circumstance with ease.

5. Straw Man – This is another type of misrepresentation or mischaracterization of an argument. Basically, the straw man is when a team set up an argument (which you have not made, and don't intend too) and then proceed to rebut it.

This might happen when a speaker uses an extreme example of your idea, when they distort anything you stated, or when they expected you to argue a specific way but instead presented something slightly different. It doesn't matter why; it's critical to call out when a team isn't engaged with your case, since if you let a straw man argument be hammered to death without pointing out that it wasn't your argument in the first place, a weak adjudicator might conclude it was. It's also crucial to point out when your opponents aren't participating, as this is a vital element of having a productive argument.

Chapter 8.
English Debate Education I

"Television"

Kids can watch TV whenever they want.

What do we know about television (TV) and kids? We all already know that TV has its good and bad sides. TV can be very entertaining and educational, but also addictive and harmful. It also has positive effect on kids; learning different cultures and influence by role models motivating for positive lifestyle changes. However, watching TV kids are exposed to negative health behavior or habits. Addiction to TV lead kids to be isolated from social community.

There are 3 parts of debate.

1) **Before the debate.**

- Brainstorm the topic
- Critical thinking
- Research the topic (both pros and cons)
- Writing reasons and evidences (both pros and cons)
- Writing an essay (introduction/body/conclusion)

2) **During the debate.**

- Teams decide a first turn by flipping a coin
- Teams take turns by giving speeches of agreement or disagreement
- Crossfire 1
- Rebuttals
- Crossfire 2
- Summary
- Grand crossfire
- Final focus

3) **After the debate**

- Evaluation of the debate
- Result of the debate

Before the debate.

1) Brainstorm the topic

What is Brainstorming?

The basic definition···but wait···there's more···

So what do we choose?

(K.I.S.S.) − keep it seriously simple

- Brainstorming is coming up with many ideas (new, old, good, "bad") about a topic or challenge
- It should involve coming up with ideas that are not al- ways traditional or "what we always do"
- Brainstorming realizes that our brains are "pattern rec- ognition systems" and that we can get "stuck" − so we need not be confined to a box

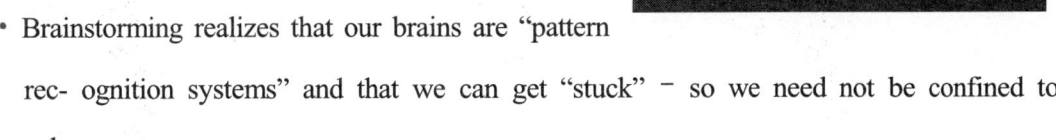

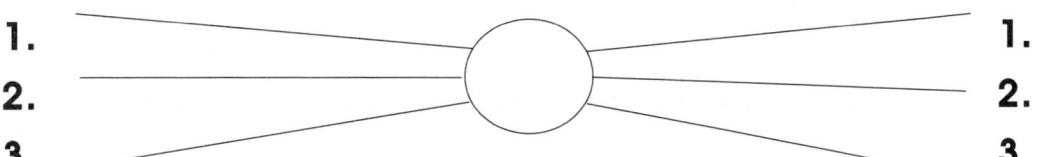

Reasons	Supporting Ideas
1.	1.
2.	2.
3.	3.

Chapter 8 English Debate Education I

2) Critical thinking

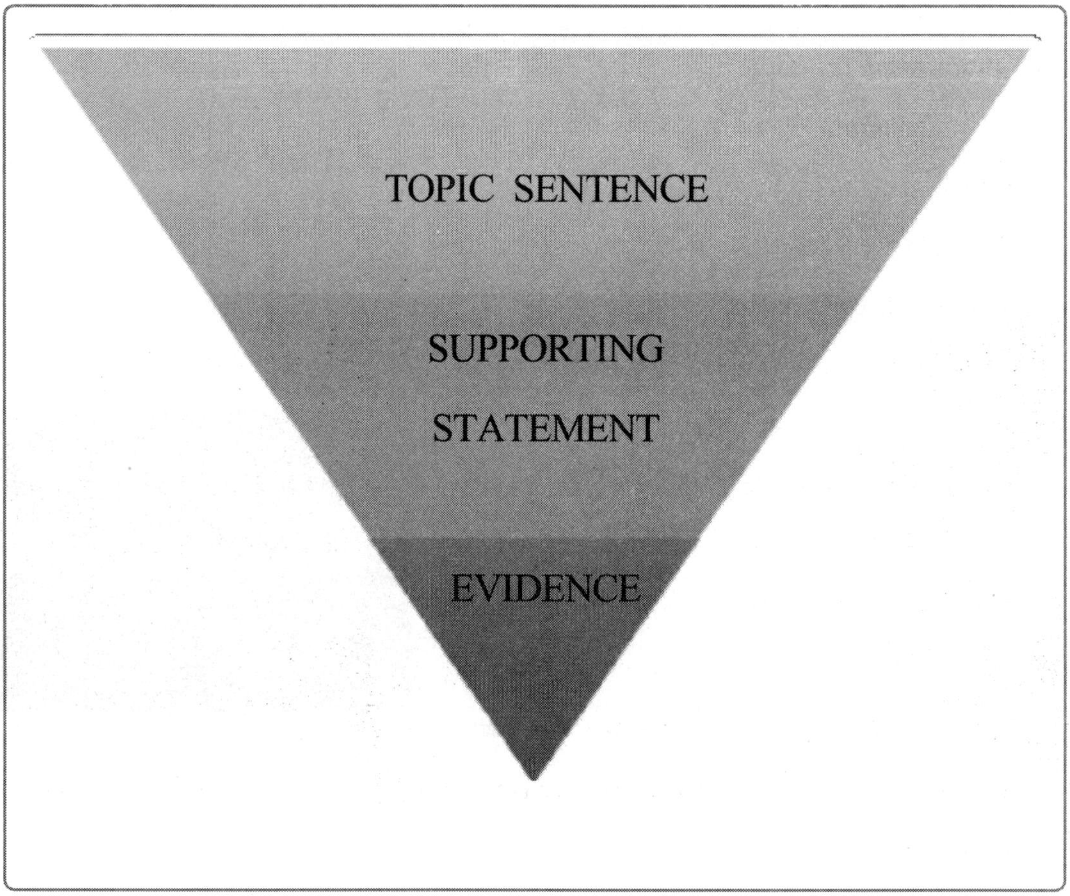

TOPIC SENTENCE
SUPPORTING STATEMENT
EVIDENCE

There are 4 critical questions you need to think about.

Idea
Why?
Evidence 1
Evidence 2
Evidence 3

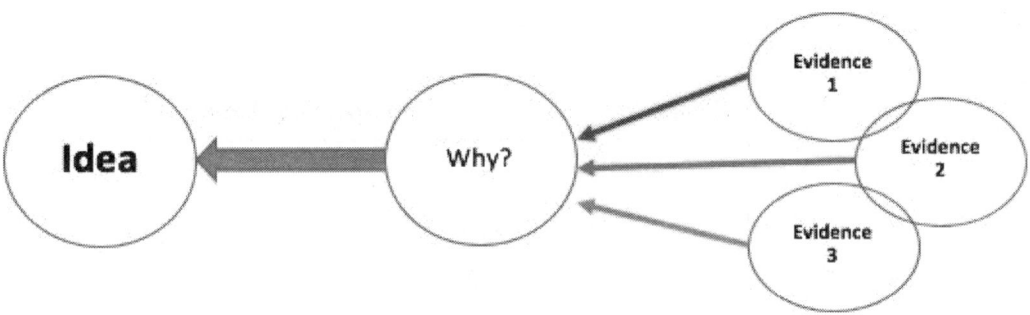

Why do you think TV is good or bad for kids?

3) Research the topic (both pros and cons)

Importance of debate:

- Arguments has to be based on evidence, facts and statistics
- Debater becomes familiar with the topic, that creates a better flow of expressing ideas and better preparation for rebuttal arguments
- Over-research

Looking for information

- **Internet**

> Online databases

> *Current information (online newspapers, articles, studies …)*

> Blogs, Wikis, and websites of concerned organizations and societies

- **Library**

> Books

> Periodicals

> Government documents

> *Newspapers*

> Videos/DVDs

- Writing reasons and evidences (both pros and cons)

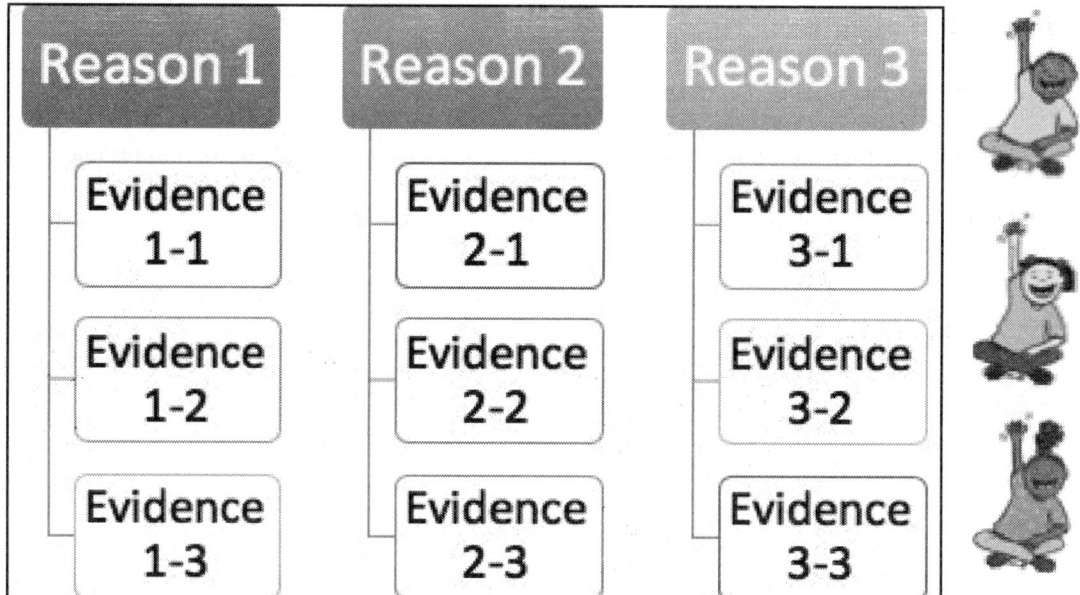

- Writing an essay (introduction/body/conclusion)

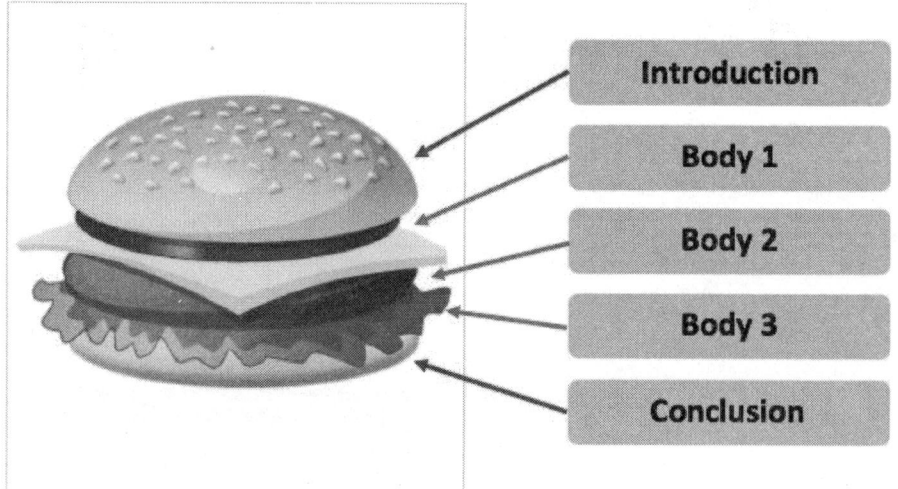

Chapter 9.

English Debate Education II

During the debate.

- Teams decide a first turn by flipping a coin
- Before we start the debate, the judge will flip the coin to decide which team is for or against and, which team begins the debate.
- Teams take turns by giving speeches of agreement or disagreement.

1) Crossfire 1

In crossfire, both debaters have equal access to the floor, but the first question must be asked to the debater who just finished speaking by a debater from the other team. After the initial question and answer, either debater may question or answer. In the first two crossfires, only the corresponding speakers may participate, and they stand next to each other.

2) **Rebuttals**

- It is a refuting of your opponent's proposals/arguments:

The goal of refutation is to answer your opponent's arguments:

1. Identifying the particular argument you are refuting
2. Critically evaluating the argument and explaining why it is wrong
3. Supplying additional evidence to support your claims.
4. Explaining the implications of this particular argument for the more controversial issue.

3) **Summary**

- These are complicated speeches because each debater has to find a way to explain issues in the light of all that has happened so far ‑ in just two minutes ‑ without speaking too rapidly. New evidence, but not new arguments may be presented, except responses (refutation). This means that a limited number of issues can be addressed. For example, perhaps develop one to two issues from the debater's side on the resolution and one from the opponent's side of the resolution. The speech should have a brief overview. On each key argument, try to add a short original quotation, anecdote, or fact. Wrap up each argument by stressing its importance in arriving at a fair decision.

4) Grand Crossfire

- Seated, all debaters interact with one another. The first question is asked to the team that just ended its summary by the other team. After the initial question and answer, any debater may question or answer, and all should participate. The same guidelines for rudeness and stalling ap- ply to the grand crossfire. Resist rushing questions or answers, or trying to do too much in cross- fire; desperation is not persuasive.

5) Final Focus

- This frames, with clarity, why your team has won the debate. Again, no new arguments may be presented, however, new evidence may be introduced to support an argument made earlier in the debate. Before the final focus, ask, "If I were judging this round, what would I be voting on?" Strategies may include:

★ Choose the most important argument you are winning, and summarize the analysis and evidence that make it so important.

★ Turn a major argument from your opponent into the winning analysis and evidence of one of your important arguments; this technique clinches two arguments.

★ Answer the most important argument you may be losing by summarizing the analysis and evidence that you believe takes out the opponent's argument.

★ Choose an argument that you believe the community judge will most likely vote on.

★ Expose a major inconsistency made by your opponent—two arguments that contradict each other—at least one of which the opponent is focusing on to win the debate.

The debate is followed by a certain format:

Speeches and Time Limits

Speaker 1 (Team A, 1st speaker). ·················· 4 min.
Speaker 2 (Team B, 1st speaker). ·················· 4 min.
Crossfire (between speakers 1 & 2). ·················· 3 min.
Speaker 3 (Team A, 2nd speaker) ·················· 4 min.
Speaker 4 (Team B, 2nd speaker). ·················· 4 min.
Crossfire (between speakers 3 & 4). ·················· 3 min.
Speaker 1 Summary ·················· 2 min.
Speaker 2 Summary ·················· 2 min.
Grand Crossfire (all speakers) ·················· 3 min.
Speaker 3 Final Focus. ·················· 2 min.
Speaker 4 Final Focus. ·················· 2 min

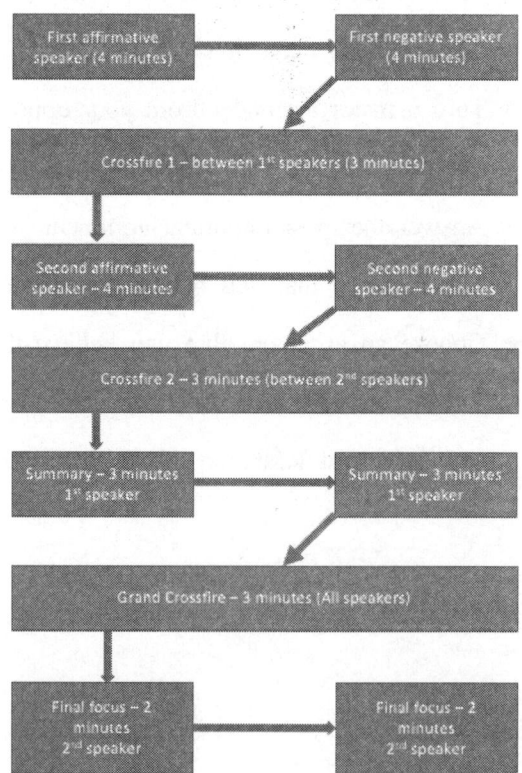

After the debate

1) Evaluation & Judging

- The judge is the chairperson of the round (facilitating the coin flip and giving time signals if requested), and may halt any crossfire lacking civility. S/he may not interact in the crossfire. Judges evaluate teams on the quality of the arguments actually made, not on their own personal beliefs, and not on issues they think a particular side should have covered.

- Judges should assess the bearing of each argument on the truth or falsehood of the assigned resolution. The pro should prove that the resolution is true, and the con should prove that the resolution in not true.

- Teams should strive to provide a straightforward perspective on the resolution; judges should discount unfair, obscure interpretations that only serve to confuse the opposing team. Plans (formalized, comprehensive proposals for implementation), counter-attacks and critics (off-topic arguments) are not allowed. Generalized, practical solutions should support a Quality, well-explained arguments should trump a mere quantity thereof.

- Debaters should use quoted evidence to support their claims, and well-chosen, relevant evidence may strengthen - but not replace - arguments.

- Clear communication is a major consideration. Judges weigh arguments only to the extent that they are clearly explained, and they will discount arguments that are too fast, too garbled, or too jargon-laden to be understood.

Chapter 10. Tips for Judging a Round of Public Forum Debate

The Role of the Judge

Each debate round will have a judge who will decide which team does the better job of debating. The judge is instructed to base his/her decision on the arguments made in the debate round, not on his/her personal beliefs about the issues. Usually, a judge will take notes and do his or her best to follow all of the arguments you make. At the conclusion of the debate, the judge will write a ballot which explains his/her decision. You will get your ballot back at the end of the tournament.

1. Before the debate

✦ Find out the exact wording of the debate resolution and write it down.

- ✦Read and follow the instructions on the judging ballot you will receive.
- ✦Read the PFD Judge Instructions that are provided for you.
- ✦You may introduce yourself to the debaters before the debate starts, but without showing favoritism toward either side.
- ✦Debaters should always be respectful of one another and of you, and you should set a tone of decorum.

2. To begin the debate

- ✦There will be a coin toss to determine the side and the speaking order that each team will take in the debate. The team that wins the toss may choose either the side or the speaking position it prefers. The team that loses the toss makes the remaining choice.
- ✦The team that speaks first in the debate should be listed on the left side of the ballot and sit on the left side of the room as you, the judge, loot at the debater.
- ✦Please pay close attention when recording the team code and side. You can ask teams for this information again of you are uncertain.

3. During the debate

- ✦Judges need to monitor speaking times during the round. Maximum speech times are listed on the ballot. Each team has two minutes of preparation time total in each round to use before their speeches.
- ✦Judge should not ask questions or otherwise interrupt the round.
- ✦Debaters directly questions each other only during the Crossfire segments, with the team that spoke first asking the first question.
- ✦Debaters should not expect any response from the judge.
- ✦Judges are advised that plans and counterpanes by either team are not allowed and that the Final Focus must deal only with issues previously raised in the debate.

✦Judges should be objective and judge the debate on the quality of the arguments made, not on personal beliefs or on the arguments you wish they had made.

4. After the debate

✦Please pay close attention to the side that each team chose in the debate and which spoke first and last. Check your codes carefully. This is especially important when marking the winner of the debate.

✦Judges should not reveal their decision at the end of the round.

✦In your written comments, please be as encouraging and educational as possible.

✦Assign points between 20 and 30, indicating the quality of each team as indicated on the ballot.

✦Checking your ballot carefully before you turn it in. Did you:

✦Declare a winner

✦Assign team speaker points

✦Provide useful suggestions for improvement

✦Justify your decision thoroughly

✦Justify your decision thoroughly

✦Sign the ballot

ORIGINAL ORATORY BALLOT

Student name _____ Round _____ Section _____

School _____ Judge name / Affiliation _____

Type of speech _____ Length of speech _____

Topic _____

Category	Description	Points(circle)				
Introduction	Did the introduction catch your interest and clearly indicate the belief and/or action that the speech would support?	5	4	3	2	1
Content	Was the speech clearly organized?	5	4	3	2	1
	Were there effective transitions between ideas?	5	4	3	2	1
	Did the speech contain compelling reasoning and clear evidence of critical thinking by the speaker?	5	4	3	2	1
	Did the speaker provide evidence, examples and/or analysis to support the ideas expressed?	5	4	3	2	1
	When used, were sources appropriately cited?	5	4	3	2	1
	Was the word choice selective and discriminating?	5	4	3	2	1
Delivery	Was the speaker's delivery fluent, natural and communicative?	5	4	3	2	1
	Were unmotivated gesture, random movement and artificial vocal variety avoided?	5	4	3	2	1
Overall Effectiveness	What was the total impression of the speech and speaker upon you, the critic, as compared to other speakers in the round?	5	4	3	2	1
	TOTAL					

Circle the number below that indications the rating of this speaker. Ties are permitted.

EXCELLENT				GOOD				FAIR			
50	49	48	47	44	43	42	41	36	35	34	33
46	45			40	39	38		32	31		

Comment

Rank the speaker compared to the other speakers. No ties are permitted.

1   2   3   4   5   6   7

Public Forum Ballot

Tournament Date:			Tournament Location:	
Round/ Flight:	Room:	Division:	Judge Name:	Affiliation/ Occupation:
Resolution/ Topic:				

Every round begins with a coin toss; the winning team has the option of choosing either the side (pro or con) or the speaking order (first or second) in the round; the losing team makes the remaining choice, either side order.
After the coin toss, record the following (the team on the left speaks first and should sit to the

judge's left):

First team		
Code:	Side: Pro ( ) Con ( )	
Speaker 1 Name:		
Speaker 3 Name:		

Second Team		
Code:	Side: Pro ( ) Con ( )	
Speaker 2 Name:		
Speaker 4 Name:		

Rate each speaker. < 20 Unethical/ Inappropriate Behavior 20-23 Below Average 24-26 Average 27-28 Above Average 29-30 Outstanding

Winning Team: Pro ( ) Con ( )	Team/ Code:

- ❖ Judges should decide the round as it is debated, not based on their personal beliefs.
- ❖ Debaters should advocate or reject the resolution in manner clear to the non-specialist citizen judge (i.e. jury). Clash of ideas is essential to debate.
- ❖ Debaters should display solid logic and reasoning, advocate a position, utilize evidence, and communicate clear ideas using professional decorum.
- ❖ Neither the pro nor con is permitted to offer a plan or counterplan, defined as a formalized, comprehensive proposal of implementation. Rather, they should offer reasoning to support a position of advocacy. Debaters may offer generalized, practical solutions.
- ❖ Crossfire time should be dedicated to questions and answers rather than reading evidence. Evidence may be referred to extemporaneously.
- ❖ No new arguments may be introduced in the Final focus; however, debaters may include new evidence to support prior arguments.

Comments to debaters:

Comments to debaters:

Order/ Time Limits of Speeches
Speaker 1_____4 min.
Speaker 2_____4 min.
Crossfire(1&2)_____ 3 min.
Speaker 3_____4 min.
Speaker 4_____4 min.
Crossfire(3&4)_____ 3 min.
Speaker 1 Summary_____ 2 min.
Speaker 2 Summary_____ 2 min.
Crossfire(all)_____ 3 min.
Speaker 3 Final Focus_____ 2 min.
Speaker 4 Final Focus_____ 2 min.
2 minutes of prep time per side
● The first question is asked by the earlier speaker.

Reasons for Decision (cite specific arguments that had a bearing):

Comments to debaters:

Comments to debaters:

Comments to debaters:

Comments to debaters:

Reasons for Decision (cite specific arguments that had a bearing):

Order/ Time Limits of Speeches

Speaker 1 _____	4 min.
Speaker 2 _____	4 min.
Crossfire(1&2) _____	3 min.
Speaker 3 _____	4 min.
Speaker 4 _____	4 min.
Crossfire(3&4) _____	3 min.
Speaker 1 Summary ____	2 min.
Speaker 2 Summary ____	2 min.
Crossfire(all) _____	3 min.
Speaker 3 Final Focus __	2 min.
Speaker 4 Final Focus __	2 min.

2 minutes of prep time per side
- The first question is asked by the earlier speaker.

Chapter 11. Practical Teaching Methods in Debate Classes

Possible activities in each part of debate

[Components]

- Paraphrasing & Summarizing

I. Opening Statement

- Impromptu Speech
- Role Play {Brainstorming}
- Four Corner (O / X) Debate {Brainstorming}
- Inner & Outer Circle Debate
- Cause-and-effect
- Making a wall Magazine

II. Rebuttal

- Jigsaw Puzzle / Information gap
- Note-taking
- Making Point-Refutation cards

III. Summary

IV. Crossfire

- A ball game / Analyzing the speech

V. Final Focus Speech

- Compare & Contrast
- Persuasive speech

1. Opening Statement

I. Impromptu Speech

① Statistics [★note]

- Support your points, but
- Be prepared to back them up with various sources
  - Cite your evidences and sources
  - Make a good balance between arguments and evidence (→ a good mix with statistics only when needed)

② Statistics [sample structures]

- One-third of the students use their computer…
- A 75% majority have/has voted against…
- According to a 2010 Kaiser Foundation study quoted on the President's Council on Fitness, Sports and Nutrition web-site, 8- to 18-year-olds spend more than 7 ½ hours a day in front of TV, video games and computer screens despite the recommendation of… 1 to 2 hours for 3- to 18-year-olds.

③ Quotations [sample structures]

- Louis V. Gerstner, Jr. says, "Computers are magnificent tools for the realization of our dreams, but no machine can replace the human spark of spirit, compassion, love, and understanding."
- To quote John F. Kennedy, "Man is still the most extraordinary computer of all."

④ Personal Narrative (Experience)

- Pro : Health risk/_____?_____

    Q: If you used a computer for about 6 hrs, how would you feel?

- Con : Learning aids/_____?_____

    Q: If you were asked to find the country's childhood obesity rates, how would

⑤ Triple Speak

Teacher presents 3 different colored cards with words faced down

Person	Students	Adults	Children
Place	Classroo	Office	Home
Thing/Act	Screen	Watch	Read

- Students select 3 cards in different colors
- Students connect 3 dissimilar words into coherent sentence/speech (story)
- Rotate the class

II. Role Play

- Teacher presents a debate question with index cards

cf. index cards: leader debater/questioner/responder]

- Teacher divides Students into a group of 3 members
- Students take their role by choosing the card
- Students with the same role get together
- Students come up with ideas {Brainstorming}
- (Back to their own group)

- Each group discusses on the issue

III. Four Corner (O/X) Debate

- T creates 4 signs (Strongly Agree/Agree/···) & places each sign in 4 corners of class
- Students take a stand on the issue
- Students move the corner of the classroom where its sign is posted···
- Students come up with ideas/words {Brainstorming}
- Students write them on cards

IV. Inner/Outer Circle Debate

- (After Students take a stand on the issue)
- T arrange Students into 2-lined circles of chairs
- Inner S (pro) & outer S (con) face to face
- Inner S proposes their ideas
- Outer S take notes of their partner (inner S)
- Take turns

V. Cause & Effect

- T presents a debate question
- Students take a stand on the issue
- (After Pro. & Con. Grouping)
- Each group come up with ideas {Brainstorming}
- Fill in the diagram/organizer/ T-chart

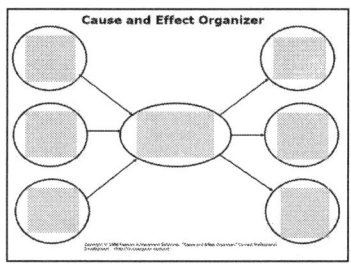 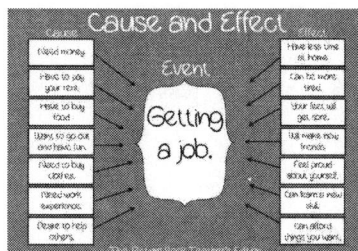

> **Key Points : 3 Strategies to Teach *Cause-and-Effect***
> ① **Asking Questions** [i.e., "Why did it happen?" / "What happened?"]
> ② **Identifying** Special (Qualifier) **Words** [i.e., as a result, because, probably, etc.]
> ③ **Using Visual Representation** [i.e., single event / branching tree] → [see Template]

VI. Making a Wall Magazine

* Evidence Cards Checklist:

★ What makes an excerpt a good piece of evidence?

_____ **Relevance:**

_____ **Authoritative:** cites a credible study, gives strong reasoning

_____ **Presentability:** short enough to be read in a debate

_____ **In Context:** should not change the meaning the author intends

★ What **included** in a full source citation? It consists of :

_____ Author

_____ Author's Qualifications

_____ Publication (name of periodical, book, or report)

_____ Date of Publication

_____ Page Number(s) / Name of Computer Service or Network

★ What makes a **good tag (headline)** for a piece of evidence?

_____ **Summarizes the main idea** of the excerpt accurately

_____ Uses **powerful** and descriptive language

_____ is 6 words or less

2. Rebuttals

★ Jigsaw puzzle / Information gap
    (with Flow-Chart)

★ Note-taking (with Flow-Chart)
  - Pick up key words (#, verbs, nouns)
  - Abbreviate
  - Write down in shorthand

★ Making Point-Refutation cards

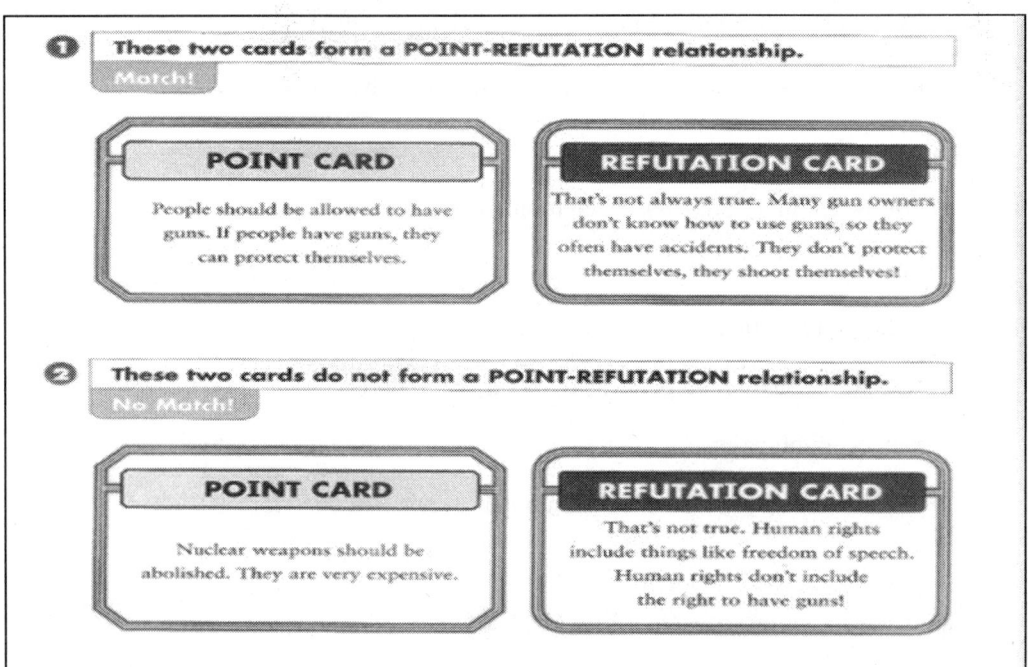

3. Summary

: Enumerate their arguments

: Long sentences → Short sentences

　★ Paragraph → 5 Sentences + Conjunction.

　★ Dictogloss

　　　- 1st member : Pick up S + V in paragraph

　　　- 2nd member : Add 1 word (adj. or noun)

　　　- 3rd member : Add 1 word to make a full sentence

　　　　⇒ Read aloud to the other team & Check if they understand it

Difference between Paraphrasing & Summarizing

Paraphrasing:	Summarizing:
■ A restatement of an author's idea.	■ A series of restatements about an article, essay, etc.
■ Length of restatement can be as long as or longer than original.	■ Restatements work together as a whole.
■ Paraphrasing is a fundamental part of writing a summary.	■ Summary is much shorter than original.
■ Change to different sentences.	

4. Crossfire

: Test the arguments of the opposite team through Q&A

★ A Ball Game

- Making questions by throwing a ball for taking turns

★ Analyzing the Speech

- Watching a video clip & Making questions about the content.

5. Final Focus Speech

: Synthesize their arguments into 1 critical point [refer to III. Summary Section]

★ Compare & Contrast

- Making a statement using T- Chart (from the opposite team's arguments)

★ Persuasive Speech

- Selecting 1 important argument to convince the audience of your viewpoint.

• Three Main Persuasive Approaches:

1. Ethos: appeals to the audience's ethics or morals

2. Pathos: appeals to the audience's emotions

3. Logos: appeals to the audience's logic or intellect

Chapter 12.
Discussion About Effective Teaching English Debate Classes

Language of today

- As a discussion class, I would like participation and input from all.
- I think ⋯ , in my opinion ⋯, I believe ⋯
- I agree / I disagree, that's so true, I have to side with (name) on this one
- What do you think? How do you feel about that?

What is a Debate?

a Noun - a formal discussion on a particular topic in a public meeting, in which opposing arguments are put forward.

The degree of structure and formality is up to the teacher. There are usually two teams of at least two people each. One team, the affirmative, supports the resolution. The second team, the Negative, opposes it.

What is effective teaching of English?

imaginative / immersive
interactive / engaging
meaningful / memorable
creative / strategic

The motion of a debate

- "Debate classes are an effective way of teaching English."

- Already Defined Debate

- Already Defined effective English teaching

We've set the motion in motion.

Teachers Role in Debate

- Provide topic and resources
- Facilitate brainstorming and skill building
- Help organize information
- Provide time and formal setting

NBC News: 65 year old woman has a baby.

SHOCKING!!
Everyone has an opinion on this topic but is that the only reason to consider a topic?

Control

Choosing a topic

- What makes a good topic for debate?
- in an English classroom?

Students should be allowed to concentrate on English skills.

Chapter 12 Discussion About Effective Teaching English Debate

Good topics for debate

- that it be some current interest and significance to young people and to students;
- that it have two opposing sides or points of view, each with identifiable arguments;
- that it not be too narrow or limited in its range or applicability;
- that it be worded in the affirmative;
- that it not deal with sectarian religion or party politics explicitly;
- that it be clear and unambiguous in its wording.

Topics to be used in parliamentary debates are called resolutions of bills, as such they begin with the conventional opening.

- Impromptu debate resolutions are also worded in the parliamentary manner as above, though the tone of the debate and the judging criteria will differ significantly; for example: Garbage cans come in different sizes.
- Cross-Examination topics are always framed as questions that can be answered affirmatively or negatively; for example: Would it serve a useful purpose for the next premier of Quebec to be an Anglophone?

Debating topics come in three different types or categories:

① Fact: A debate about the correctness of an objectively verifiable statement. This types of resolution can only work if the evidence is not clear-cur and conclusive.

② Value: An appraisal of the relative merits of one object, idea or action as opposed to another; for example: Dogs are better than cats.

③ Policy: A dispute which argues that a particular course of action be followed, or not be followed. It starts with the examination of the relative value of the course of action, but must also deal with how the Government plans to carry their proposal.

Brainstorming / Skill building

- why - builds confidence in the students
- how - defining the motion is one example
- other examples - vocabulary check, 3rd party opinion

> Provide enough information for all students to partake.

Help organize information

- why - builds confidence in the students
- how - defining the motion is one example
- other examples - vocabulary check, 3rd party opinion

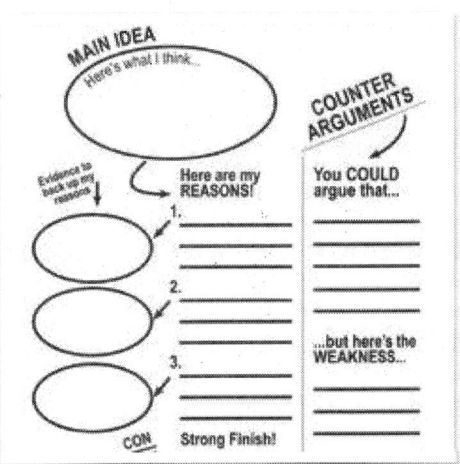

> Students can reference each others opinions, not rely on memory

Provide time and formal setting

- Debate structure allows time for consideration of language
- imitate formal settings of debate: court, university debate room, parliament

Students Role in Debate

- Research topic and review material.
- Define material as affirmative, negative or irrelevant. Establish argument and defense.
- Understand the other side's argument, plan rebuttal.

Difference between students

- The traditional way to define students of English is by level
- low-level, mid-level, high-level

level-based development

low-level   mid-level   high-level

o Research topic and review material.
o Define material as affirmative, negative or irrelevant.
o Establish argument and defence.
o Understand the other side's argument, plan rebuttal.

Research topic (motion)

- The motion should provide the main focus for debate
- Level consideration: language development, vocabu- lary and grammar, comprehension.
- Research examples: newspaper/internet articles, sci- entific research, statistics, expert opinion.

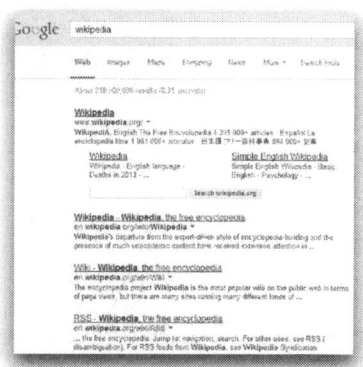

Review material

- Testing understanding of the topic:

> Material should be defined as positive or negative to the motion, either by students (high-level) or by the teacher.

- Low-level: sentence / definition matches. Mid-level: sentence completions.
- High-level: sentence constructions.

Establish argument and defence

- Test writing and reasoning skills:
- Low-level: single simple sentence
- Mid-level: sentence with different connectives
- High-level: multiple sentences, structured.

Understanding the other side

- Low-level: speech template based on other side
- Mid-level: rebuttal based on other side
- High-level: Persuasion based on other side

Debating has rules

- rules make debating perfect for a constructive class with active participation.
- The teacher is able to control discussion (use of English) in the classroom, like a judge in a court.
- Instructors prepare each lesson with objectives appropriate to the setting and goals of their class.
- These objectives may range from the learning of specific vocabulary to broad conceptual content.

Role-play in Debate

- A fantasy setting for the debate to take place
- court
- parliament

Judge/Teache

affirmative   negative

Provide language to add to the authenticity of the place

benefits teacher by choosing quiet students in talking roles, and control chatty students.

- Language can help
- court
- parliament

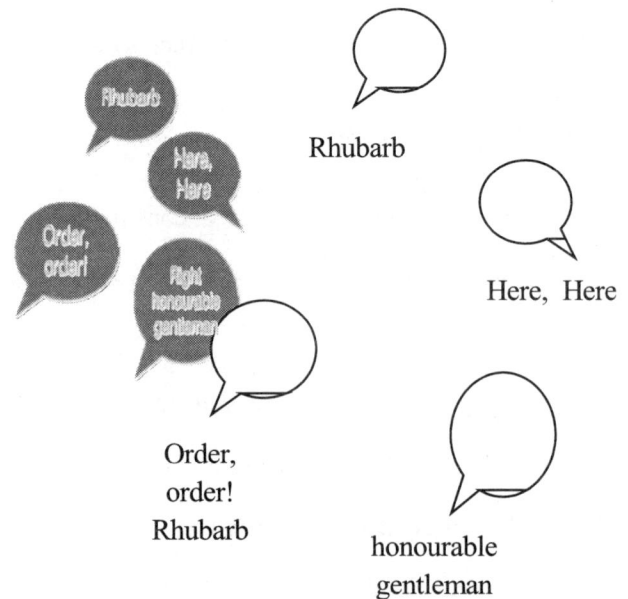

Rhubarb

Here, Here

Order, order!
Rhubarb

honourable gentleman

Assigning roles in debate

- Traditionally 1st speaker, 2nd speaker, 3rd speaker
- low-level: argument, rebuttal (single sen- tence)
- Also: note taker, adjudicator, Judge

Visualize the debate

- Provide students with large graphic handouts they can fill in to explain their position.
- Allows both teacher and other students to follow the debate.

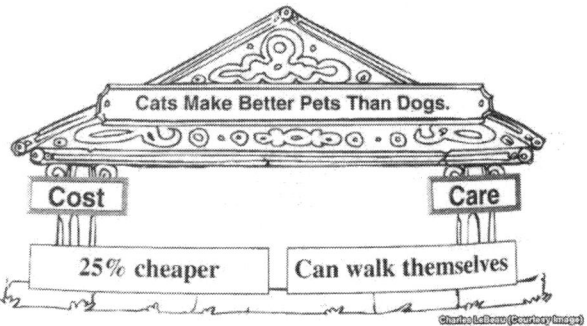

Illustration: Discover Debate, Professor Charles Lebeau and Michael Lubetsky

The "Discover Debate" approach has three stages: creating a visual aid to communicate an argument, presenting the argument and answering the other team's argument.

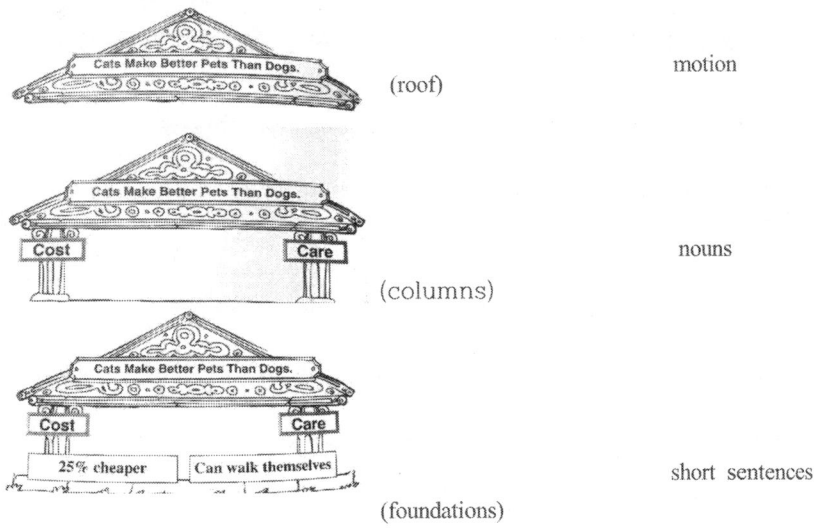

(roof) — motion

(columns) — nouns

(foundations) — short sentences

Chapter 12 Discussion About Effective Teaching English Debate

Comment or question

- provided students with 2 or 3 cards titled either "comment" or "question"
- students must use the card when they want to ask a question or make a comment in the debate.
- Teacher able to monitor who talks and stop some students talking too much.

Debate as English Class

- prepare students for their future language needs
- defining words
- meaningful language use
- authentic text
- adaptable to needs of the group
- debate relies on communication toward an audience.

Which Language Skills Are Improved During Debates?

- Speaking skills - improve oral skills with appropriate phrases and structures.
- Listening skills - students listen to one another carefully and understand their points of view.
- Writing skills - students take notes and write their arguments.
- Reading skills - students preparing their arguments by reading articles and web-sites.
- Critical thinking in the foreign language is enhanced. Every step encourages students to use logic in discussion and express their ideas.

Chapter 13.
Coaching Debating

Anyone who teaches can be a good debating coach. The popular conception that debating coaches can be teachers of English or perhaps history is entirely false. Debating starts with a large members of common sense, and we all have that. The only prerequisites are a genuine enjoyment of working with bright young minds, an interest in ideas and a commitment to effective, lively communication.

1. How should I coach debaters for a particular debate?

Debating is education. Math teachers never write their students' tests for them – they leave that to the students. So the debate coach keeps his or her distance from the debaters, too. It is a obsolete to the students to "do it for them." So I would suggest this procedure:

- A tournament resolution and conditions are received in advance. Call a meeting of all those interested in taking part.
- Set up the teams; complete the registration from and mail it.
- Hold a brainstorming session on the resolution, and on its possible interpretations and definitions. Encourage and assist the debaters by writing ideas on the board or remembering them.
- Discuss fruitful lines of research. Indicate possible sources.
- Keep them on their toes before you have arranged to see them next. "How are you getting on with that affirmative case? What definition did you decide to use."
- Before the tournament, you do not need to criticize logical contradiction or weakness in either case – each team will discover these when they face their "in-house" opposition. Shine a big light on them; show them the way, but don't do it for them.
- Ease off before the tournament. Do not pressure debaters at the last minute. They have either done what they need to do or they have not – it's too late to do much about it.
- And when you return to school, after it's all over, hold a postmortem. Help your debaters to benefit from their experiences; discuss the strong and weak points of their recent oppositions, ask them what comments they received from judges. It all adds up to a better performance next time.

2. What should be the goals of my coaching?

You should encourage your students in these directions:

To achieve an overview of the subject, details find their place later.

To be flexible in their response to an opponent's arguments, to ensure that their constructive speeches are replies – a debate should be a logical conversation in four parts.

To despise tactics which involve falsification of facts or a deliberate misquotation of an opponent.

To be modest; success in debating, like nuclear physics, can release huge amounts of potential energy. Bombastic debaters are the bane of organizer's lives. Let us have tournaments without mushroom clouds.

3. What is expected of me by other coaches and organizer?

It boils down to the Five Musts;

① Be responsible: If you enter three teams, arrive with three teams; if you are to bring three judges. If you have to cancel a team, do it as soon as you know. Turning up a team short is unforgivable.

② Be on time: For your registration deadline. And for the tournament.

③ Control your debaters: Most debaters need no "control", but we can all think of some who do. You are responsible for your debaters' manners, punctuality, and appearances.

④ Supervise your students: You must supervise your debaters at all times or make arrangements for them to be supervised.

⑤ Have a sense of humor.

What about things to avoid?

① Debate coaches do not unfair for a certain team in debate.

② Debate coaches do not complain.

③ Debate coaches never intervene in any way during a debate.

Chapter 14.
Establishing a Debating Programme

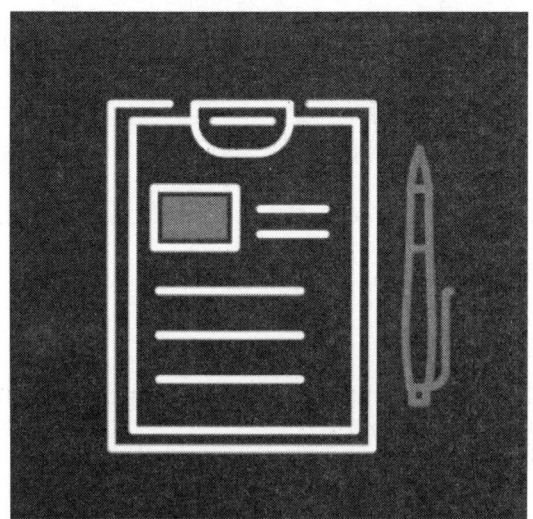

1. Developing Critical Thinking Skills

Some debate events are organized so that students must argue both sides of an issue during the curse of the event. This can broaden student's approaches to all issues. Their evaluative and discriminative skills are developed as well.

Development of critical thinking skills has an application outside of debate or school, often providing experienced student debaters with a perspective and problem-solving edge over their peers.

2. Honing Research Skills

Though it is sometimes assumed that students can adequately learn research skills through normal curricular instruction, class size, time and other limitations make this prospect extremely unlikely.

The debate club or debate option approach allows more flexibility for the one-on-one or small group interaction necessary to develop research skills.

3. Speaking Skills

Mistakenly, people think of the terms "debate" and "public speaking" as synonymous. The term "public speaking" often assumes style is of greatest importance. In proper debate, content research and logic are of equal (if not greater) importance than the style of public speaking.

The public speaking aspect is, however, a contributory factor to the quality of a debater's skill, and therefore, when taken in its proper perspective, serves an important educational purpose in debate.

4. Stimulating Internet In and Understanding of Issues

Debate involves the in-depth study of contemporary social, economic and political issues.

5. Bringing the School Recognition

Though a secondary benefit and not recommended as a sole objective, debate as a viable extra curricular activity casts a positive light n the opportunities offered by a particular school.

When all these objectives are emphasized in their proper balance, it is found that the developments of an unusually high level of maturity, leadership and camaraderie among participants tends to occur. It involves the in-depth study of contemporary social, economic and political issues.

6. Organizing a Debate Program

If the school is so fortunate, a true option program can be established within the curriculum. Students in the option, as well as the teacher, are able to involve themselves outside of class, having had greater time and emphasis within the class.

Because this is not always the case, we should look at the practicalities involved in developing an extra-curricular club.

In most cases, though there are notable exceptions, the debate club rarely gains the degree of notoriety held by a winning a school. This does not mean, however, that debate cannot become a well-respected and valuable addition to a list of extra-curricular choices that normally emphasizes non-academic pursuits.

Remember, debating is extremely valuable for directly developing skills that complement that curriculum and the personal development of participants.

Chapter 15. Managing a Debating programme

To run your programme as a club, you need to organize the election of a basic executive to provide organization and leadership, and in so doing to take work and responsibility off your shoulders. Here are some guidelines for roles and responsibilities for your debate club executive:

President:

- chairs meetings;
- consults with staff coach(es);
- plans impromptu debates;

- receives members' concern and questions;
- raises issues of club concern;
- helps coach(es) construct tournament teams;
- reminds executive members of their duties;

Vice-president:

- assists president as needed in the above duties;
- takes a turn charing a meeting.

Secretary:

- issues all notices of meetings;
- keeps and distributes copies of all important mail, especially tournament invitations;
- responds to all mail or memos as directed by the membership;
- makes sure that debating communications are effective.

Treasurer:

- collects and records any money from fundraising or other sources;
- keeps all monies secure until submitting to the coach.

Meet weekly on the same day in the same room, if possible. If no external debating event is coming up, use meetings to hold impromptu, informal debates so the students can get their feet wet, to see how they feel about the activity and to get to know each other. Encourage the members to submit topics to the president for future debate. At an early stage, it's very important to stick to the club principle: allow the executive and membership to run the show, with your support when needed.

If your region has planned a novice workshop for the fall, that will be the first external event you get notice of. Plan on entering as many club members as are allowed. There won't be anything at stake, and the objective will just be experience and fun. Encourage the hesitant ones with that message. If such a workshop is not taking place in your region, then ask our regional coordinator to introduce one. It's a proven way to start the debating year, but the competitive element must not be prominent.

As each tournament notice arrives, different styles (Parliamentary, Cross-Examination and Impromptu) will need to be introduced, demonstrated and practised. When competition dates get closer, you will want to plan research teams to go to the library and out to the larger community to garner information and opinion to be shared with teammates. This is an important stage in the club's functioning, when a sense of sharing and team cooperation starts to be built. Clear communication of plans at this time is crucial. You should consider, or your president should, holding two or even three meetings a week.

Chapter 16.

A Debating Worksheet

Plastic surgery can improve your life.

Yes(for)   No(against)

You will be part of the group that is **against** today's topic. Write an opening statement in agreement of the above statement.

opening statement: Against

Give 3 reasons and supports for your opinion on today's debate.

Sharp reasons: Against	Sharp support: Against
The physical traits you have are unique.	Most plastic surgery is about changing something about yourself to look less unique.

End with a summary speech concluding your opinion on the debate topic.

closing statement: Against

Plastic surgery can improve your life.

Yes(for)   No(against)

You will be part of the group that is for today's topic. Write an opening statement in agreement of the above statement.

opening statement: For

Give 3 reasons and supports for your opinion on today's debate.

Sharp reasons: For	Sharp support: For
physical enhancements can help improve self-esteem.	with improved self-esteem a person can achieve more.

End with a summary speech concluding your opinion on the debate topic.

closing statement: For

A Debating Worksheet and Model Speech (Pro)

Debater's Name: _____

Topic:

_____

Full Resolution:

_____
_____
_____

Key Words Defined:

_____
_____
_____
_____

Underlying Issues:

_____
_____
_____
_____

Relevant Resources – Human, Print, Media:

_____
_____
_____
_____

Supporting Facts:
_____
_____
_____
_____
_____
_____

Opposing Arguments Anticipated:
_____
_____
_____
_____
_____
_____

Useful Quotations, One-Liners:
_____
_____
_____
_____
_____
_____

A Debating Worksheet and Model Speech (Con)

Debater's Name: _____

Topic:

_____

_____

Full Resolution:

_____

_____

_____

Key Words Defined:

_____

_____

_____

Underlying Issues:

_____

_____

_____

Relevant Resources – Human, Print, Media:

_____

_____

_____

Supporting Facts:

___

Opposing Arguments Anticipated:

___

Useful Quotations, One-Liners:

___

Sample Parliamentary Style Speech by the Prime Minister

(Dan Wilson, Cameron Heights C.I., Kitchener on February 20, 1980)

Topic: B.I.R.T. Rural Life is Preferable to Urban Life (a value resolution)

1. Introduction

Mr. or Madame Speaker, honorable judges, patient timekeeper, members of the Queen's Loyal Opposition, learned colleague, distinguished members of the gallery: I rise in support of the resolution that Rural Life is Preferable to Urban Life.

This Government's plan of attack will be as follows: As Prime Minister I shall define the topic and deal with the social arguments of this debate. My associate will analyse the physical and economic arguments.

2. Definition

According to the 1980 voters' guide published by this government, "rural life" is defined as "existence in a community with a population of 5,000 or less." From there, we must deduce that "urban life" is existence in a community with a population of 5,000 or more, in specific and defined limits, that is, a city or town. "Preferable" is defined by the Funk and Wagnell's dictionary as "more desirable".

More desirable to whom, Mr. Speaker? Desirable to my colleague and me, less desirable to the opposition? Maybe so, but this government does not want to embark on bickering over personal preference. We wish debate that: Rural life is preferable to urban life for the majority of Canadians.

This, we hope, eliminates pointless arguments.

So with the resolution in mind and with the Speaker's permission, I will proceed.

3. Development

Argument #1

Mr. Speaker, there is less crime in rural areas. The statistics from Ontario Statistics 1975 show a direct between the ratio of a province's rural dwellers to city dwellers, and the crime rate. Ontario, with one person in the country for every five in the city, has a crime rate of 9.11%, whereas New Brunswick with three rural people for every one city person has a crime rate of only 4%. Mr. Speaker, we feel it would be preferable to the majority of Canadians to live in an area with a lower crime rate, and a rural community provides that.

Those statistics do raise some questions, however. Why would the crime rate be higher in a city, where people often use every precaution known to man to protect themselves, where the police are often just minutes away, and where people are often close by and could help? Why would the crime rate be lower in a rural community, where police are often mile away, and where it is common to see houses left alone, unlocked and unprotected?

Some say because all those devices, and the constant presence of police, create a challenge that criminals want to try to meet. We don't buy this theory. We feel that the fast pace of the city life, with clogged up traffic and the pressures of nine-to-five jobs, build up in a city dweller, and often crime is used as a release valve.

Argument #2

This brings up another point. Rural life should be preferable to the majority of Canadians as it is not as pressure filled as urban life is. In a rural community, there are wide open spaces, fresh clean air, and a special harmony not found in the city. It has to be more relaxing, and it is a proven fact that one is less likely to suffer from mental anguish and heart disease if his lifestyle is tranquil. But is urban life all that pressure filled?

Yes, according to the '78-'79 Canadian yearbook, urban centres have an average pressure-related suicide rate of .3% whereas in rural areas, that figure is 0.07%. These statistics prove rural life is not as pressure filled as urban life.

4. Conclusion

Mr. or Madame Speaker, it is for these three reasons:
- a lower crime rate
- a more relaxing setting
- choices of types of relaxation

that we feel the majority of Canadians would prefer rural life to urban life. Hence, rural life is definitely preferable to urban life.

Notes:

Chapter 17.
Criticizing Debate

Criticizing Debate

Organizing a debating tournament

When you agree to host a tournament at your school, remember that decide the work and worries you foresee, staff and students from all participating schools are always ready to help out, if you just ask. When you it's all said and done, you and your school will share a splendid sense of accomplishment. Debating is worth the effort.

Leaders:

Try to identify two or three key helpers (staff and students) so that you will be free to meet people and to attend to their concerns. A small planning committee within your school debating club could take charge of major areas as judges, speaker/timers, refreshments, and so on.

Topic/ Resolution:

A good deal of thought should go into the choice of a topic (cross-examination) or resolution (parlimentary, impromtu). Be sure that your selection is reasonably current, appropriate in difficulty for the age and experience of the students, not repetitive of past tournaments or debating events, balanced for both sides of the issue and quite open-ended.

Judging sheet:

Prepare the judging sheet and be sure to have plenty of ballots duplicated for each round. Judges are normally encouraged to write suggestions on the ballot and to offer very brief spoken comments at the end of each debate, but without giving away specific results or scores.

Officials:

Each debate (2 vs.2) requires a speaker/timer. It is reasonable to ask one student to do both jobs, but they should be provided with timer cards numbered 1 through 9, a blank script suitable for the format and a stopwatch of the rooms don't have clocks. Each school can be asked to bring one official speaker/timer for each team entered, but be sure to remind schools of this in your invitation.

Rooms:

It is important that you clear the use of your school with your principal, and inform the debate competition plans and needs. Select rooms that are central, easy to set up for a debate and that can be opened by a regular staff key, if possible.

Matchups:

It is best to wait until the last minute before doing your tournament pairings, because of last minute entries and withdrawals. This will give you valuable flexibility. Above all, avoid one school debating against itself, and don't let any judge hear the same debaters twice: it's bad for both parties. Basically, all you need to do is to list all participating schools vertically, separating "A" and "B" team from one school by at least two spaces. Then slice them one line for Round One opponents, and slide them again for Round Two opponents. If in doubt, call on one of the many "veteran" coaches around or the coordinator.

Results:

Choose a small room near the judges'/coaches' lounge where tabulation will be done. Have at least one teacher/coach in charge and offer a student to help with the calculations, particularly the checking of the addition on the judges' completed ballots.

Have a summary sheet or sheets drawn up that indicate horizontally the schools, the four team members' names, Round One score, totals and final standing.

All addition should be double checked, but time should be kept to a minimum. The coordinator should verify results before any announcements are made.

Perhaps a model debate, speech or performance of some kind could be put on while results are being tallied.

Judges' Instructions:

If possible, try to send out a copy of the judging ballot and some instructional materials to any judges you have recruited. Do this at least one week in advance of your tournament. This is good public relations and will improve the confidence and competence of your judges.

Chapter 18. Practicum for Teaching Debate

E-Zone Debate Class - Plastic Surgery.

Plastic surgery can improve your life.

Yes(for)   **No(against)**

You will be part of the group that is **against** today's topic. Write an opening statement in agreement of the above statement.

opening statement: Against

Give 3 reasons and supports for your opinion on today's debate.

Sharp reasons: Against	Sharp support: Against
The physical traits you have are unique.	Most plastic surgery is about changing something about yourself to look less unique.

End with a summary speech concluding your opinion on the debate topic.

closing statement: Against

E-Zone Debate Class - Plastic Surgery.

Plastic surgery can improve your life.

Yes(for)   No(against)

You will be part of the group that is **for** today's topic. Write an opening statement in agreement of the above statement.

opening statement: For

Give 3 reasons and supports for your opinion on today's debate.

Sharp reasons: For	Sharp support: For
physical enhancements can help improve self-esteem.	with improved self-esteem a person can achieve more.

End with a summary speech concluding your opinion on the debate topic.

closing statement: For

Chapter 18 Practicum for Teaching Debate

Debate class - Debate topic, Plastic surgery.

1. addiction
2. vanity
3. enhancement
4. risky
5. side-effect
6. expense
7. uniformity
8. perception
9. confidence

A. (such as a belief or a way of behaving) which shows that you have too much pride in yourself, your social status, etc.

B. the amount of money that is needed to pay for or buy something

C. involving the possibility of something bad or unpleasant happening : involving risk

D. a strong and harmful need to regularly have something (such as a drug) or do something (gambling)

E. the way you think about or understand someone or something

F. the quality or state of being the same : the quality or state of being uniform or identical

G. an often harmful and unwanted effect of an action that is not expected or intended.

H. a feeling or belief that you can do something well or succeed at something

I. to increase or improve (something)

Sample Debate

1. Should teacher be replaced with computers?

<pro>

In the last decade, technology has placed many careers on the chopping block: travel agent, photo processor, even to some extent postal clerk. Most of teachers are confident in their job securities, have never had to worry. However, some student's don't learn well in classroom. They distracted far too easily or cannot learn fast enough, for computer software help here as students can work at their own pace. Sure, using technology in the classroom allows you to experiment in pedagogy, democratize the classroom and better engage students.

Firstly, robot teachers can accelerate the schedule of teaching if not programmed or formatted well. They are followed up by the artificial intelligence which is nothing but an alternative or substitution of human basic reactions – something which the robots have imitated through the research and development phases. Then it can also have speakers to talk. In those science fiction shows where the computer has like a zigzagged wave going across it. Computers would have that soon with our technology getting better.

Secondly, personally I feel a lot is still required to replace human teachers with Robots. Research is going on to make it them common in the classroom settings, which definitely is a hell lot challenging than situation programmed in their robotic system. Like a projector a computer could have one with it so that it projects what a human could do. So like a holographic teacher controlled by the computer. It could be the exact same as a teacher.

Lastly, this is can be possibly a good-way to refer to live tutoring for the online courses or e-learning programs, if candidates are to select the odd hours. But that should be for a temporary period, maybe just to quickly refer to the FAQ's of adult learners. Like this the kids will treat it like games, so then they will pay more attention to class. They would say like this. "This is part of my homework please tell me how I can do it." Then the teachers might lose their jobs easily because they are as smart as their teachers for a lot of subjects.

People are relying on technology more and more. Computers can be programmed, so those people that say they have no feelings you can program them to know and have feelings. Teachers are dependent on computers too. It takes time for teachers to get the technology set up for a lesson, if it were a computer it can automatically do it itself. People are creating better and better technology, it wont be long until a computer can program its self like a person can control itself.

\<con\>

Technology gives children the ability to learn in ways their parents and grandparents never had. Today's learners have immediate access to answers and research. Yet, that immediate access is changing the way students think about work and how they feel emotionally. Teacher is more like a friend who not only open the door to the realm of education but also is the tour guide in the reality. While a computer is just a machine that represent an information board. The teacher knows how to bring the best to students.

Firstly, human beings have different behavioral and psychological levels that defines their social skills and interactivity. A teacher can quickly discover and adjust to his or her student's learning curve. By so doing the teacher dictates what the learner requires and when they require it especially so in terms of information or facts. This may be a near impossible task for a computer to carry out however complex the computer program may be.

Secondly, teachers have 'unique' social skills and cognitive ratio exclusively found in humans. Learning also involves response and feedback. Sometimes the learner's response is erratic and unplanned and can only be well interpreted by a human. To effectively have a program up and running to decipher all the unplanned and erratic feedback would mean a complex and very expensive computer program.

Lastly, computers are expensive, so not every school or student will be able to afford a computer of their own in the classroom. In most schools, students will have to share one computer per a group 5-8 people. However, teachers can give you more of a personal one on one. Also computers will give you the answer but will not show you how to get it, or explain it. Unless when governments change their policies towards education and use tax payers money to buy equipment needed in the classroom. It is mainly private schools that provide these facilities to each student.

Technology provides students opportunities to engage efficiently and effectively with ideas and individuals, but it cannot replace teachers. A computer would not be able to provide discipline, safety or care for a child. Sitting our children in front of a computer to learn all that they need to know will take away critical human interaction which our children need. Computers should be used as a learning tool, not as a teacher. Sara Eskridge, history professor at Randolph College in Virginia, believes that technology is a tool to be used in the classroom, rather than an end in itself. It can, however, liberate those teachers to assume a potent new role in the facilitation of that learning process.

Sample Debate

2. Are video games good for you?

<pro>

Do video games really hinder our ability to learn, make us more violent, or affect our physical health? Some say it is in our human nature to find something to blame when there's an issue, and video games have always been an easy target. But things have changed and now more professional studies are being conducted to find out the truth. While there still isn't enough evidence to offer a solid answer, the good news is that most researchers are discovering that games can be good for us.

First, video games may slow down aging. While getting older and wiser has its perks, there are also a number of natural problems that come about as well. In fact, a study conducted by researchers at the University of Iowa showed that playing games can do just that. The study had 681 healthy people aged 50 and older play 10 hours of a certain video game for five to eight weeks, and this is what they found.

Secondly, it helps to be a better decision maker. Playing games demand us to view and keep track of moving peripheral images, improve our ability to receive sensory data and thus help us make more precise decisions. C. Shawn Green from the University of Rochester wanted to see how games affect our ability to make decisions. It shows that the group of young adults with no gaming experience play an action game for 50 hours. On the other hand, the second group of the same age played a slow-paced strategy game instead.

Lastly, games improve focus and attention. One of the biggest worries among parents today is that their children sit in class thinking about games instead of listening to the teacher.

Vikranth Bejjanki performed a few experiments alongside several colleagues. These tests first involved having two groups, experienced and inexperienced gamers, perform several perceptual tasks such as pattern discrimination. The gamers ended up outperforming the other group who rarely, if ever, played games before the experiment. In other words, playing games improves several abilities, including paying attention.

Just like video games themselves, the field of studying how games help or hurt us is still very new. There is still plenty of research to be done before we find out how the virtual characters, stories, and worlds we love really affect on a physical and mental level. It will help them realize that instead of giving us problems, games may have actually been improving our lives in some

\<con\>

With more than 90 percent of American kids playing video games for an average of two hours a day, whether that's a good idea is a valid question for parents to ask. Video games, violent ones especially, have caused such concern that the issue of whether the sale or rental of such games to children should be prohibited was brought before the Supreme Court. While violent videogames may promote some complex problem solving and coordination skills as well, they have multiple negative effects. Here are three related to moral functioning.

First, in violent video game play the player learns to associate violence with pleasure rewards for hurting another character. This undermines moral sensitivity. Under normal conditions, human emotional wiring is designed to abhor violence and feel rewarded for helping others. Those who play violent video games build opposite intuitions that they take into the rest of life.

Second, children practice over and over the actions available in a game. The player practices violent behavior hundreds if not thousands of times, much more practice than normal activities receive. Whatever a person practices repeatedly becomes an automatic response. Violent games teach children how to behave like a criminal and to intentionally hurt others.

Third, video games can be addictive because they give immediate rewards for learning. Child and adolescent brains are typically susceptible to addictions as their brains are under development till the middle 20s. Recent brain research is suggesting that any addictive behavior can harm the final stages of brain development in young adults, leaving them with a less than mature decision making system and diminished empathy for others.

The evidence is conclusive for the negative effects of violent video games. Craig Anderson and colleagues have been studying violent media for decades. They and others have found short and long term negative effects of watching or playing violent media that include increased aggressive thoughts, feelings and behavior, and decreased prosocial behavior.

Sample Debate

3. Should girls join the military?

<Pro>

Although there are some major differences between genders, like men have more physical strength than women, strength alone cannot be deciding a factor. As a matter of fact, the strength that really matters is strength of heart and mind. Lady Officers can be as physically fit as the men with the help of training. Women are capable of incredible things, including feats of physical strength, athleticism and tremendous bravery. I have always been a strong supporter of equality for women, and women in the military are no exception.

Firstly, women should be allowed to join the military even if people think its a man job to be a soldier. Women might be to "weak" to join the military could be one of your points in saying why they shouldn't be allowed entry into the armed forces. Women aren't weak even if they contain less testosterone then man, they could still be able to shoot a heavy duty weapon if needed to. Their more than mentally capable of shooting even if they have many mixed emotions.

Secondly, women should join the army because women are human they want to defend their country every one want to defend their country. Women can be more stronger than what you think! If they want to. It does not mean that they are women they are not allowed to fight. As long as an applicant is qualified for a position, one's gender is arbitrary. It is easy to recruit and deploy women who are in better shape than many men sent into combat. It is possible to calibrate recruitment and training standards to women. Extra pre-training for muscle building can also be used to reduce female injury rates. In modern high technology battlefield technical expertise and decision-making skills are increasingly more valuable than simple brute strength

Lastly, it is no excuse that women shouldn't be allowed in army because they need to care of their children or because the child needs their mother or something as it is quite obvious that a child needs a father too. They say that women have some soft corner but they can be hard when they want too. People have stated about who would be the civilians then to them men can. In the modern world of combat: Afghanistan, Iraq, all women serving in the military are exposed to "front-line risks". Support for women serving in the armed forces has not wavered as warfare has changed, a clear sign that the necessity of women serving in combat is recognized.

Women should be allowed to join the military even if people think its a man job to be a soldier. Women might be to "weak" to join the military could be one of your points in saying why they shouldn't be allowed entry into the armed forces. Women aren't weak even if they contain less testosterone then man, they could still be able to shoot a heavy duty weapon if needed to. Their more than mentally capable of shooting even if they have many mixed emotions.

<Cons>

Military is supposed to be the men's world. It was so for thousands of years. But these days this state is starting to change. More and more women, applauded by the media, join all branches of the military. One would say it's natural evolution and that the world is changing. I can't disagree with this claim. But are those changes going in the right direction?

Health is a very important factor when talking about women. During the period, women are more in hygienic conditions than usual. While in the field they not always can be met. Sometimes periods are painful and limit woman's mobility, sometimes hormones can also have influence on woman's ability to make credible decisions. It doesn't have to happen but it might and stress can only make things worse.

Another problem is sexual harassment. It happens quite often. Females will always be seen by males as sexual objects, regardless of them wearing uniform or not. If you place them in an isolated environment of military bases, there will always be some twisted mind that will try to take advantage of the situation. The only way to prevent it from happening is not to give soldiers any occasion for sexual harassment by not putting women among them.

Personal fitness is the last problem. The enemy won't ask if you are a man or a woman. The hill won't be lower, the mud less wet nor backpacks lighter if you're a female. The idea behind PE is to make sure that one soldier will be able to save life of another soldier, no matter how heavy he is. In the military everything has its purpose. It's not hard to imagine a situation where a woman have to help a wounded male soldier, especially if keeping in mind what's going on in Afghanistan.

Simply, just like not all are designed for men, not all jobs are designed for women. There always are some exceptions but they only confirm the rule. Wrongly understood equality of sex shouldn't be a reason for ignoring facts. For the greater good some things just should not change.

Sample Debate

4. Is peer pressure beneficial or harmful?

<pro>

Peer pressure is the phenomenon wherein we tend to get influenced by the lifestyles and the ways of thinking of our peers. Peer pressure can prove beneficial but it is most often observed to have negative effects on society. However, Peer pressure is useful since it makes us more alert, we can improve own-self and attentive to the happenings around us even the small ones that we might look over but actually be helpful for our knowledge and development. Also, when our peers or classmates are good at studies and other activities it motivates us to match their performance. It is certainly good if we are careless and lazy.

First, peer pressure can help you analyze yourself and contemplate on your ways of life. Some of the practices that the masses follow may actually teach you the way of living. You may be able to change yourself for the better. Looking at what others do, can help you bring about a positive change in your way of thinking. If you can pick selectively, peer pressure can actually result in a positive change in your way of life.

Second, knowing what the masses follow exposes you to the world outside your home. You understand the things going on around you. You are exposed to a wide variety in human behavior. Exposure to peer pressure gives you an opportunity to think about their tastes and their outlooks towards life. It gives you a chance to choose the best from what the masses do.

Lastly, it may influence you to change for betterment. If you are fortunate to get a good peer group, your peers can play a vital role in the shaping of your personality. Some of your peers are your close friends, who do not pressurize you to do things but rather inspire you to change yourself. Your peer group may actually persuade you to bring about a constructive change in your personality. Peer pressure can lead you to make the right choices in life.

Good peer pressure is being pushed into something that you didn't have the courage to do or just didn't cross your mind to do. It also can help us analyze ourself and contemplate on our ways of life. Some of the practices that the masses follow may actually teach us the way of living. Being with a peer group can change our overall view of life from negative to positive and turn pressure into motivation, a positive force which will push us in the right direction.

\<con\>

We tend to get influenced by the lifestyles of our peer group. The changing ways of life of our peers often force us to change our ways of looking at life and leading it. Peer pressure is the phenomenon wherein we tend to get influenced by the lifestyles and the ways of thinking of our peers. Peer pressure can prove beneficial but it is most often observed to have negative effects on society.

Firstly, Peer pressure can lead to a loss of individuality. Extreme peer pressure may lead you to follow what your peers feel right. Their pressure may compel you to go by everything they think right. You tend to blindly imitate the masses; you adopt their tastes of fashion, clothing, hair, music and general living. Peer pressure can actually lead you to lose you tastes of life and force yourself to begin liking what they like.

Secondly, peer pressure leads a negative lifestyle. it may make you do all that you had never wished to. There are many teenagers who experience great pressure from their peer group that forces them to take to drinking. You may take to something as grave as drug use, and that too, only because of peer pressure. In such cases, being overly pressurized by you peers can be detrimental to your living. Some teenagers literally spoil their lives by giving in to peer pressure.

Lastly, it may compel you on doing something you hate. In such cases, there are chances that you won't do well in those things. Things you do not enjoy doing cannot fetch you success. When you do not like a particular idea or when you have no inclination towards a particular field, it is obvious that you won't like to go by it. You cannot emerge successful in something you have never liked doing. So, it is important that you do not lose happiness of your life by succumbing to peer pressure.

Teenage is that phase of life when you are exposed to the world outside. These are the years when you spend most of your time with your friends. Teenage is the phase of beginning to become independent in life; the years of forming your ideals and principles, the years that shape your personality and the years that introduce you to your own self. Therefore, they need to be taught to distinguish between the good and the bad, the right and the wrong and should be taught to be thoughtful in life. Their pressure may force you to go by everything they think right. Peer pressure can actually lead you to lose your tastes in life and force yourself to begin liking what they like. The person loses his/her original way of looking at life. This makes the conclusions that, before following your peer, think about the impact.

Sample Debate

5. Is using animal for clothes bad?

<Pro>

Imagine living in a cage for your entire life, in poor conditions, with no food and water. Then you are suddenly ripped from your cage, beaten to near death, and painfully skinned alive. Your body is then tossed into a pile, like a piece of garbage, with others who have suffered the same fate. Each year, millions of animals are tortured and killed wrongly for the fur on their backs. The fur trade is a heartless business that is cruel, unnecessary, and bad for the environment.

First, it's a lot more harmful to the environment than one would think. Since fur will naturally decompose with time, the fur companies apply massive amounts of chemicals to the pelts to keep them from rotting, such as ammonia, formaldehyde, chromium, and hydrogen peroxide. These are all hazardous to humans. Also a lot of the fur companies like to promote how they're eco-friendly, but it takes more energy into producing a fur coat then a synthetic one.

Secondly, making animal furs is too much cruel to support that industry by buying fur, especially when it's not even necessary. For starters, fur is not necessary for survival. Everyone can live without it. Also, there are many other stylish alternatives that are as aesthetically pleasing and as warm as fur. Fabrics such as polyvinyl and polyester are common cruelty free clothing materials. Not only are these synthetic fabrics stylish, but they are also a whole lot cheaper than buying fur.

Thirdly, people in cold climates should be able to wear fur coats to keep themselves warm. Real fur as a fashion though, shouldn't be allowed. Some people though need to wear fur so they don't get hypothermia outside! Also, in the meat industry it would be okay to make fur, as it would be wasteful to only use one part of the animal instead of making as much use as possible for the animal's death.

Environmental factors aside, killing animals for fur is completely wrong. It is a brutal industry where the lives of many innocent animals die in the name of fashion. There is no point to making them suffer because fur is not an essential part of life. They don't have a voice, but we can speak for them by refusing to wear fur or refusing to buy from companies that sell fur.

The most obvious benefit of a real fur coat is that it can keep an individual warm when it is cold. These garments also tend to make positive statements about wearers, the exception being that wearing a such a coat can enrage animal rights supporters.

<Con>

Using animal fur for clothes is an ethical dilemma that many people raise questions. However, most people agree that if animals are well-treated, there are few possibilities of becoming extinct, none of the animal is wasted, and the animal is put to good use. Furthermore, they have been using for humans in many ways since prehistoric ages, so it is acceptable for us to use and consume them.

Firstly, Fur has always been a good idea to wear; a lot of people have been wearing it for years. Since the look is glamorous, many designers have chosen as a material of clothes. The young have preferred to wear it, for it is a little bit edgy, something a little bit different for style.

Secondly, banning fur and leather is too much of an invasion of human rights. In some climates only animal skins will shield you from the harsh weather. So banning fur and leather should not be acceptable. Furthermore, it is common to eat meat, so it is unfair to ban to use fur or leather. Then, maybe all of us should have to be vegetarians. Anyhow, raising animals for food has also raised some concerns, both environmental and about animal cruelty.

Lastly, animal goods have been worn by people for thousands of years. So, it is not acceptable to ban fur and leather. They are actually better for the environment than wearing other artificial materials. While animal lovers might not be happy with the wearing of fur and leather, others would not mind wearing fur or leather.

In conclusion, making a fuss about fur is hypocritical. Society is fundamentally okay with eating meat. Animals are not treated as such wrong in clothing industry, but you don't see PETA: People for the Ethical Treatment of Animals in any markets. So, it is okay to wear leather or furs in shoes and clothing.

Sample Debate

6. Tattoos and piercing

\<pro\>

Society has become pretty open minded when it comes to diversity and personal expression in the workplace. For many employers, the appearance of tattoos on employees is undesirable, especially in client-facing roles. For decades, tattoos and other forms of body art have been connected to a not-so-clean lifestyle. The Harris Interactive poll stated that 50 percent of people without tattoos perceive those with tattoos as more rebellious or capable of deviant behavior.

The first is to manage the perception that clients and other employees may have about tattoos on workers. Many are still conservative and find tattoos offensive. Therefore, it is acceptable to create a workplace policy that requires employees to cover their tattoos in a reasonable manner. So, tattoos should be covered up while on the company's time.

Secondly, teens are more impulsive and more likely to engage in risky behaviors. More than one third of the people who get a tattoo regret it, and they're three times more likely to regret a tattoo they got before they turned 16. Studies show that the tattoos most often regretted are those gotten on an impulse, or after a night of partying. The last part of the brain to develop is the part that tells people to put the brakes on before they do something risky.

Lastly, there's also a serious risk of infection associated with tattoos. Unsanitary tattooing practices can expose teens to germs and bacteria that cause serious skin infections, such as staph infections, tuberculosis and hepatitis B and hepatitis C viruses. Tattoo artists should use sterile needles and razors, wash hands, wear gloves and keep all surfaces clean to protect their clients from the risk of infections.

\<con\>

Body piercing and visible tattoos are frowned upon and often go against the rules and regulations of that establishment at many schools and more professional workplaces. Personally, I feel that a person is entitled to look as they wish and that having holes in their body or ink in their skin shouldn't impact their professional life. Obviously there are exceptions to this, such as if someone had a very visible offensive tattoo, such as a form of racism, but in general I don't think piercing and tattoos should be much of an issue.

Firstly, it is a great way to express oneself in a specific way and to make your self-image more individual. People also use tattoos and piercings, but mostly tattoos, to remember someone or something in their lives. Tattoos for family, friends or a special event are common to keep sentimental memories. Because tattoos and piercing are a form of expression, then why do so many people have a problem with them?

Secondly. tattoos are irrelevant to how a person performs and most importantly how they do their work. I would say know the story before you judge people and their ink. It could have a deep and meaningful meaning like me. It took a lot of courage for me to know that I was getting something tattooed on me for the rest of my life. So, I see no reason to ban.

Thirdly, Tattoos is defining Mark for Millennial. Tattoos are one of the few evidences of a true generation gap. Just 10% of those over 40 years old admit to a tattoo. Thirty-six percent of Millennials and 40% of Gen X have at least one tattoo and many have multiples. It's clear that Generation X and Y are leading the trend toward acceptance of body art in the workplace in a big way.

In conclusion, tattoos should not be viewed negatively. They are a part of a person's sense of culture, an expression of oneself and to judge them is to judge the person. Plus, tattoos are a freedom of expression, but I don't think they should be viewed negatively. Therefore, tattoos are not, and never will be, an indicator of talent or skillset an individual has.

Sample Debate

7. Do our neighborhoods define who we are?

<pro>

How do our neighborhoods make us who we are? How much do they define us and the way we see the world? How do they shape our personality or impact our future? These are some of the questions we want to explore. A 2010 study, The Mechanisms of Neighborhood Effects Theory, Evidence, and Policy Implications, found direct links between a person's neighborhood and factors like health, education, and personal outcomes.

Firstly, it does have a small factor on the schools that children can attend and the amount of peace that a family can have; however, some people choose to have a higher quality of life experiences and do not want to spend their time working extremely hard to just pay for a house in an extremely nice neighborhood. Having the opportunity to live in a peaceful neighborhood with good schools can transform lives.

Also, people who are forced to live in inner city life are more susceptible to bad decisions because thats just the neighborhood that they live in. They're many facts supporting the idea that your neighborhood defines exactly who you are and how you act in society as well as the choices you make. Also stated in Professor David Kirp's article, "Those who didn't secure housing report that their neighborhoods remain pockmarked by violence.

The problem is not the people nor the neighborhood, it's societies view of people in poverty. They put this pressure on them to act a certain way and they must live to it. People in poverty don't get out, which is why they neighborhood you live in will define you and generations after you as well. We need to stop putting generalizations on low-income individuals and provide them with the tools they need to have a better life.

Where you live can really impact who you are. Where you grow up and the lifestyle you live plays a huge part on who you become. The environment surrounding you contributes to what you do and your view point on certain things. The viewpoint, life experience, surrounding and poverty of someone who grew up in neighborhood with a higher education will be very different

\<cons\>

The neighborhood that you live in does not completely define who you are. I agree that it does have a small factor on the schools that children can attend and the amount of peace that a family can have; however, some people choose to have a higher quality of life experiences and do not want to spend their time working extremely hard to just pay for a house in an extremely nice neighborhood.

Firstly, you are not defined by the area that you live. As long as you have the things that you need to be successful in life, you will be defined by the people that you surround yourself by and how you carry yourself.

Also, some people are born in a family that is less fortunate and that may not live in the most extravagant of a neighborhood, but they do not let that define who they are. I believe that if you work hard and are willing to put in the effort that you can succeed no matter where you live as long as you are provided the adequate resources.

Another reason that where you live does not define you is because some people would rather spend their money on experiences instead of a large mortgage for a house in a 'nice' neighborhood. I think that these are the experiences that define you as a person; the amount of time you have spent soaking in other cultures, seeing the world from more than one perspective and getting a feeling for how other countries work.

The neighborhood in which you live ultimately does not define who you are. I believe that you are defined by the people you surround yourself by, the way one carries themselves as a person, as well as the experiences that you may have throughout your life.

Sample Debate

8. Should students be physically punished by adults?

<Pro>

A 2008 study on the effectiveness of physical punishment on children in the U.S. found no long term effects on behavior change; essentially, when the threat of punishment was gone, the negative behavior returned. Therefore, corporal punishment is a good tool for disciplining unruly children, and also it can ethically help save a child's future. Corporal punishment is the most effective way of maintaining school discipline and dealing with juvenile crime.

Firstly, corporal punishment allowed It should be allowed because some children needs discipline to be able to behave well. According to Bnet, the undeniable fact is the 'uncivilized' practice of whipping children produced more civilized young people. In that 'uncivilized' era, assaulting a teacher or adult never would have crossed our minds. Today, foul language and assaults against teachers are routine in many schools.

Secondly, it gives these children structure, it also keeps them behaving and not disrespect their teachers or any adult for that matter. It should be allowed as long as its necessary and not taken out of context. I dont see any issues with corporal punishment. If my child were not behaving in class I dont have an issue with a paddling.

Lastly, corporal punishment can ethically help save a child's future. Today, it's not uncommon for young criminals to be arrested, counseled and released to the custody of a parent 20 or 30 times before they spend one night in jail. Such a person is a very good candidate for later serving a long prison sentence or, worse, facing the death penalty. So, which is more cruel: caning or allowing such a person to become a criminal?"

Corporal punishment is designed to punish specific acts of significant misbehavior and delinquency. It is not a wanton and unreasonable act of violence. Child abuse, on the contrary, is the unjustified and unreasoned beating of children. The act of child-abuse is not meant to punish a child, but is inflicted without restraint or concern for the general welfare of a child. The intention of corporal punishment, on the contrary, is meant to instill a level of discipline in a child that is necessary to their future.

\<con\>

Researchers define physical punishment as "the intentional infliction of pain and discomfort and/or the use of force to stop or change a behavior." Additionally, there is extensive research that physical punishment puts children at substantial risks for future defiant and aggressive behavior, increased mental health concerns, as well as greater risk of serious injury and abuse.

Firstly, children learn to behave when their parents notice and respond to their behavior appropriately. When a child misbehaves, it is essential that parents remain calm and communicate the appropriate way to get it right next time. If adults use corporal punishment freely for changing children's behaviors, vicious cycle will be continued.

Additionally, there is extensive research that physical punishment puts children at substantial risks for future defiant and aggressive behavior, increased mental health concerns, as well as greater risk of serious injury and abuse. Recent brain science research has shown that harsh physical punishment may actually have detrimental effects on the development of a child's brain.

What's more, consistent use of punishment in schools causes children to become fearful and avoidment of school and teachers, and interferes with positive, pro-social relationships. The risks to physical punishment are huge and well outweigh the short term reduction of a negative behavior.

Brain science is showing us that warmth and nurture are essential to brain development. Academic success is best achieved in a school climate that is warm, welcoming, and promotes positive behavior and positive interactions with adults and peers. It's time to change the culture of discipline in our country, and to show parents that there is a better way. Rather than debate its effectiveness, let's educate on its tremendous risks, and on more positive approaches to discipline.

Short activities and exercises

Debates and other types of Speaking & Listening exercises don't have to take a long time to prepare, nor do they have to take up a whole class period. Quick activities like hat discussions and rebuttal tennis can be used as excellent openers or brief portions of other lectures. Use these as a warm-up before a debate lesson to get everyone "in the zone."

Hat debates

A hat debate entails the selection of very basic motions from a hat. Often, there is only one speaker in favor of the topic and one speaker opposing it. Participants have little (or no) time to prepare for the discussion, so it's excellent practice for thinking on your feet. Here are some motions that would be appropriate for a hat debate:

- We shouldn't have to wear school uniform
- Girls and boys should go to the same schools
- You should be allowed your mobile phone in school
- SATs should be abolished
- PE should not be compulsory in schools
- It's a good thing that London won the bid for the Olympic games
- Violent video games should be banned
- Policemen should carry guns
- Books are better than television
- It's better to live in the countryside than in a city
- It's a waste of time to learn foreign languages
- It would be a good thing to be famous
- Footballers earn too much money

- English is the best subject at school

Rebuttal tennis

The term "rebuttal" refers to instances in a debate where participants disagree with what their opponents have said. Short bouts of "rebuttal tennis" can be used to hone this talent. Students are seated in pairs, with one making a pro statement and the other instantly disagreeing. The first student then disagrees... Who will be able to keep going the longest?

- Here are some light-hearted topics for fun games of rebuttal tennis.
- Valentine's day should be abolished
- We should have a national Harry Potter Day
- EastEnders is the best soap opera
- We should have video games as a subject in school
- Justin Timberlake is a good role model for young boys
- Britney Spears is a good role model for young girls
- Cartoons should be banned
- Levels of pocket money should be set by the government
- Teenage magazines talk too much about sex
- Women should stay at home and look after the children
- Footballers earn too much money
- Compulsory PE should be banned in schools
- English is the best subject at school
- You should be allowed to choose all your GCSE subjects

You can [broken link]watch our video of primary school students from Hackney playing Rebuttal Tennis.

Chapter 18 Practicum for Teaching Debate

Mamamoo

This game improves nonverbal communication. The teacher selects a student and conveys a sentiment to them (sad, happy, shy, angry, surprised, scared, cheeky, disappointed, confident, excited etc.). The student must transmit the emotion to the group or class, but they can only say "mamamoo" or some other nonsensical phrase; therefore, they must employ facial and verbal expressions, as well as body language. The group has to figure out what emotion is being expressed. You can advance to new circumstances to enhance the difficulty (saying sorry, asking for directions, proposing, teaching a class, telling a joke etc.).

Emotional counting

This activity improves nonverbal communication. The teacher selects a student and instructs them to count from one to ten while altering their emotion as they go, for example, beginning at one with "happy" and gradually increasing up to ten with "sad." Because the student is unable to communicate the change through words, he or she must rely on voice and facial expressions, as well as body language.

The "Um-err" game

The goal of this game is to improve fluency. The student is given an easy topic to discuss (my school, my family, animals, television, sport etc.). They each have sixty seconds to speak about their chosen topic. They will receive sixty points if they speak for the entire sixty seconds. But every time they say "um" or "er" they lose a point. So, a student who manages to speak for 45 seconds and does 8 ums and ers receives 37 points. The game to be widened to include banned words such as "like", "basically", "innit", "you know" etc to encourage the use of formal English.

I couldn't disagree more...

This easy practice helps you develop the ability to think on your feet and respond quickly. The teacher (or student) makes a point, and another student is invited to answer, beginning with "I couldn't disagree more because..." and expanding on their reasoning. The statements can be silly or serious, related to the curriculum, current events, or school issues, or completely random, such as "We should brush our teeth every day," "Cats are better than dogs," "War is always wrong," "We should get rid of our school uniform," "Goldilocks was a very naughty girl," and so on.

Glossary of Policy Debate

- **Debate round** - This is a whole debate. Two teams of two debaters compete in this event. The affirmative team was referred to by one of the participants. The opposite group was dubbed the "negative team." The round's winner is determined by a judge. The speech given by each debater on each side is used to identify him or her.
- **Constructive** – The first speech is presented by every students (debaters). The time depends on structure of the debate that is conducted.
- **Rebuttal** – The second speech is presented by each students (debaters). The time is given based on the structure of the debate. Students (debaters) answer opposing team's attacks presented previously and sum up one's own position.
- **Cross Examination (Crossfire)** – For instance, a three-minute question and answer period following each constructive.
- **Preparation time** – Set amount of time given to each team to prepare their speeches, usually 5-10 minutes. A team may split this time for preparing for any speeches.
- **Flowing the round** – Taking notes of speeches presented in the round. These notes also provide the student (debater) with an outline of his or her own speeches.

- **Speaker points** – Points given by the judge measuring individual performances.
- **Resolution** - The area of discussion that is subject for debate which is uniform for all high schools in the country.
- **Affirmative Team** - Debaters who are arguing in favor of the resolution. They do this by advocating a change from the present system (status quo). This change is called the plan.
- **Negative Team** - The pair of debaters arguing against the adoption of the resolution. The Negative team usually wins by proving that the affirmative plan is not desirable.
- **Definition** - What a word in the resolution means. This is usually taken from a dictionary like Webster's or Black's Law Dictionary.
- **Violation** - The reasons why the affirmative plan does not fall under (meet) the definition of the word.
- **Disadvantage** - (DA) - A harm resulting from adoption of the affirmative plan.
- **Evidence** - All published material such as books, newspapers, and magazines, used as reference and support in a debate. This includes statistics, quotes, facts, and examples.
- **Responses or Answers** - An argument which addresses an opponent's argument.

Topics for Debate

1. Homework is good for students.
2. Should coats made with dog fur be against the law?
3. Should junk food be banned from schools?
4. Should girls join the military?
5. Should school uniforms be required?
6. Are video games good for you?
7. Should pets have funeral?
8. Is peer pressure beneficial or harmful?
9. Should makeup be allowed in schools?
10. What is the permissible age for tattoos and piercing?
11. Should North and South Korea be unified?
12. Can Money Buy You Happiness?
13. Do Kids Need Recess?
14. Are social networking sites harmful?
15. How Necessary Is a College Education?
16. Should Parents Limit How Much Time Children Spend on Tech Devices?
17. Should You Go to Jail for Kicking a Cat?
18. Do Our Neighborhoods Define Who We Are?
19. Can robot replace a person?
20. Androids are better than iPhones.
21. Students should be held legally responsible for bullying in schools
22. Should ethics be taught in school?
23. Should teachers be replaced with computers?
24. Should students be physically punished by adults?